THE WORDSTAR CUSTOMIZING GUIDE

A Complete Guide To Customizing WordStar For The IBM PC And Compatibles

Stuart E. Bonney

Wordware Publishing, Inc.
Dallas • London

Library of Congress Cataloging in Publication Data

Bonney, Stuart E..
WordStar Customizing Guide, The.

Includes index.
1. Word processing 2. WordStar (Computer program).
I. Title.
Z52.5.W67B66 1986 652'.5 85-29471
ISBN 0-915381-81-8

Publisher — **John Hunger**
Interior Design — **Russell A. Stultz**
Production Manager — **Dianne Stultz**
Typesetting Supervisor — **Kay Dorsett**
Art Director — **Alan McCuller**
Manufacturing Manager — **Linda Davis**

P.O. Box 1747
Plano, Texas 75074

3 Henrietta Street
London WC2E 8LU

Printed in the United States of America

ISBN 0-915381-81-8

10 9 8 7 6 5 4 3 2

All inquiries for volume purchases of this book should be addressed to Wordware Publishing, Inc. at one of the above addresses. Telephone inquiries may be made by calling:

(214) 423-0090 in the United States
01-240 0856 in England

Trademarks

The following trademarks appear in this book:

WordStar, MailMerge, MicroPro	MicroPro International Corporation
IBM, IBM PC, PC-DOS	International Business Machines Corp.
MS-DOS	Microsoft Corporation
CP/M, CP/M-80	Digital Research Incorporated
The Norton Utilities	Peter Norton, Inc.
ProKey	RoseSoft, Inc.
Sidekick, Superkey, Turbo Pascal	Borland International, Inc.
Symphony	Lotus Development Corporation
Framework	Ashton-Tate, Inc.

Contents

Foreword

If longevity and acceptance on a broad scale are seeds from which classics grow, WordStar has earned the appellation. It has long been rated the standard of comparison among high performance word processing programs for personal computers. Furthermore, it is a working classic. Despite ballyhoo about newer programs, the familiar WordStar opening menu still flashes across monitor screens around the world more often than any other in its class.

Although purists in other classic fields may insist on preserving original form, WordStar proves that good things sometimes can be made even better. Spurred by a core of dedicated and persistent enthusiasts, the quest for revelations about internal workings of the program that can be translated into useful enhancements goes on.

Are these mere cultish diversions? Hardly. Their objective is not intellectual exercise but practical results—to improve productivity and utility on a personal level. This book will show you how. As a bonus, you will find that your efforts also have practical applications elsewhere. A growing number of popular programs, including Borland's Turbo Pascal and Sidekick, use WordStar-like command sets and will accept your customized versions in their setup routines. Imagine, you can write, program, keep notes, edit all this, do calculations and the like, all with the same set of your own personalized commands.

The notion that software should bend to needs of its users rather than the converse is not new, but its rapid spread has led to coinage of a new term describing its adherents—the Power Users. Whether you count yourself among this sophisticated group or are presently only an aspirant, this book was written for you. It is aimed at easing your passage to a most beneficial kind of WordStar mastery.

The efforts of many who assisted me along the way are gratefully acknowledged: Tom McBroom and others at MicroPro International who generously supplied a quantity of technical data; my friends John Mason of ComputerLand, who provided printer data and many expert comments, and T. H. Jones who coupled broad knowledge with the fresh viewpoint of one new to this subject; and my wife Ardene, who toiled through several reading sessions and gave me unflagging support and encouragement.

Stuart E. Bonney

1

INTRODUCTION TO WORDSTAR CUSTOMIZING

WordStar. Mention the name in personal computing circles and you will seldom fail to get a reaction. Rarely has it inspired love at first sight. Many have proclaimed it hard to learn and often out of tune with tasks at hand. Yet it is still the world's most widely used word processing program for personal computers, with well over a million copies sold. Withstanding rising competitive winds, it continues to confound soothsayers who predicted it would be swept away by newer programs. Perhaps the simple truth is that its legions of users, having climbed its steep learning curve far enough to appreciate its virtues, have remained largely unswayed.

MicroPro's late-1984 introduction of WordStar 2000 was interpreted by early reporters as a move to supersede the original, but MicroPro has given strong assurances that the old pro will remain in the line and be actively supported. Although there are family resemblances, the two programs clearly were cut from different cloth. Command sets, menus, and internal structure differ considerably. Reviewers have compared WS-2000 to a luxury automobile, bursting with conveniences and creature comforts but ponderous and slow. The original is more akin to a fast sports car—lean, muscular, and agile but demanding a skillful driver.

The purpose of this book, however, is not to argue the merits of one program over another. It has a more practical aim—to explain how you can make WordStar more responsive to your personal requirements. If you are a typical user, you very likely have tucked away somewhere a file of patches gleaned from varied sources. These canned patches, while often useful, give you little insight to alternatives if they prove unsuitable.

This book focuses on helping you understand how things work so that you can create your own enhancements. It will show you how to alter commands for fewer, easier keystrokes, how to modify and expand function key assignments, how to change all the initial editing and page formatting parameters, how to change the way WordStar looks on your monitor screen, and how to drive and extract full performance from almost any printer. In short, it will show you how to mold WordStar into a more effective personal writing tool by making the program respond in ways that are more natural and compatible with your own individual style.

None of this demands that you know anything about programming. A modest amount of study and practice may be required if you are short on experience, but results will usually outweigh efforts by a wide margin.

If you are new to the process of modifying WordStar, you will find here the information about tools and techniques you need to get started. If you are already a confirmed WordStar customizer, you will find a quantity of useful reference material, much of it not previously available. It contains maps to command and operating parameter tables, address listings, and full details on command formats and data structures.

To begin, it is useful to examine the qualities of WordStar that make it a good candidate for changes and worth the effort. First, its editing screen is still among the cleanest around, a feature appreciated by writers who feel that busy displays are distracting. The elaborate menus and tree-structured commands of many newer programs do speed up the learning process, but later they can prove irritatingly cumbersome. WordStar lets you select menus according to your level of expertise, and its commands are more direct than many programs of similar capability. For example, you don't need to shift constantly between character, word, and sentence modes; WordStar makes no distinction. Although this makes the commands more numerous and thus harder to learn, in the end it's faster to use.

WordStar saves time by doing print formatting on the editing screen rather than forcing you into a separate formatter. Its embedded format commands are a visual nuisance, but a quick Control-OD command (or simpler equivalent to be shown later) banishes them until you want them back. The program itself is fast and remarkably compact, making it possible to set up an electronic disk drive in memory without adding an expansion board if you have a 256K system. With such a setup, WordStar really hums.

It is useful for cranking out quantities of letters, memos, and short reports, but so are many competitive programs. WordStar shows its real mettle, especially when customized, as a tool for writers of longer works which may undergo extensive revisions during the creation process or which may need to meet varied composing requirements.

A fundamental reason for using a word processor in the first place is to enhance productivity and the quality of writing. To succeed at this, the program must have more than high processing power and a broad repertoire of features. Perhaps even more important, its operation should be unobtrusive, impinging as little as possible on the stream of creative thought and the flow of words onto the screen. Ah, but here's the rub. How can anything so individually unique as creativity be served adequately by a purportedly universal tool? The obvious answer is that it cannot. It could be said, then, that the ultimate worth of any word processing program is tied to how easily it can be made to meet individual needs.

This brings us to what is possibly WordStar's most important quality. Far from being inflexible, WordStar can be configured in numerous forms for widely varying needs and applications. Its developers undoubtedly intended it to be able to run on a variety of computers, to be adaptable to machine characteristics which were still evolving, and to be easy to maintain and upgrade. The program structure that was designed to meet such criteria also makes possible a great variety of modifications to program operation without altering basic program logic, meaning that almost anyone can do it.

Customizing WordStar requires information which before now has not been generally available except in scattered and incomplete pieces. It also requires attention to detail. However, the process is not difficult, nor does it demand that you become a programmer. The reward is a powerful program tailored the way you want it.

There is no one best way to customize WordStar. What may be good for one application or personal requirement may not be so for another. Our goal is not to tell you what changes or overall configurations are presumed to be best, but to explain methods you can use to satisfy your own needs and preferences. To assist you in understanding how to reach your objectives, real setups are included as examples throughout this book. Inevitably a degree of personal leaning may surface from time to time, but you will make the final judgement of what is best for you. More important, the material presented here will allow you to exercise that judgement.

THE BASIS FOR THIS BOOK

Material in this book centers on WordStar operating under MS-DOS and, more specifically, under PC-DOS on the IBM Personal Computer. It applies also to operations on work-alike machines, although there may be minor differences. It assumes that you have a good working knowledge of WordStar operations from a user's point of view and sufficient experience to know what kinds of changes to standard program configuration would be personally beneficial. Knowledge of personal computer terminology and hexadecimal notation are also desirable but not vital.

WordStar versions 3.2 through 3.3 are the focal point. Some material, such as that on function key changes, is more applicable to one version than another. The information applies also to earlier versions, but there may be individual differences, especially in the memory locations of specific functions. Once you have acquired an overall understanding of WordStar's structure, a perusal of the program using Debug or a printed dump usually will reveal where and what these differences are. How to use the tools will be covered in detail in the following chapter.

When customizing WordStar there are a few things you should bear in mind. While creating your own version of any program can be satisfying and useful, it is neither fair nor realistic to expect its developer then to provide extensive support if you run into problems. However, this is not said to scare you off. Every attempt is made here to steer you safely around any pitfalls with thorough explanations and illustrated examples.

There is a tendency for non-programmers to be intimidated by the idea of getting into the internals of a program—a feeling often reinforced by the pervasive and cryptic jargon peculiar to the field. The number of newcomers to computing reflected by the burgeoning personal computer market probably has elevated this condition to an all-time high. This is truly unfortunate because nearly anyone who persists will discover before long that most fears of this kind are groundless.

Virtually none of the many ways presented here to customize WordStar involves any change to program logic or coding. Its architects made that unnecessary by providing the needed flexibility and access points. If you make all your changes to a backup copy, as you always should, the worst you might do is to botch up the copy badly enough to require starting over. There is no way you can cause your computer to self-destruct.

A BRIEF HISTORY OF WORDSTAR

Some of the strongest criticisms of WordStar revolve around the choice of characters used to issue program commands, its less than effective use of the PC's function key capabilities, and its start-up, or default, operating configuration. Although we will cover ways to change these, it is useful and instructive to know how all this came to be.

Originally conceived and developed in the mid to late 1970's, WordStar was the first truly comprehensive and powerful word processing program for what were known then as micro-computers. (The concept of personal computing was not invented by IBM, who chose not to invade the small computer scene for several years, although with their impact on the market and massive advertising, it was they who later popularized the term personal computer.) In those days, recent historically but distant technologically, the modern computer terminal with expanded keyboard and a full set of programmable function keys was not common as it is now. Teletype machines and keyboards having layouts similar to office typewriters were widely used, leaving the control key as almost the only special key available to programmers. Thus, it was natural that this key became a principal element in the design of program commands.

With only the control key available for use with other standard keys, designers of programs having many commands soon ran out of natural mnemonic choices. Moreover, they were forced to use the control key and not one but two character keys. In consequence, WordStar commands which seem illogical or physically difficult to type were born more from necessity than poor ergonomic design, in spite of a few instances of the latter malady.

The advent of expanded keyboards has, of course, changed the picture. Many newer word processing programs make better use of the keyboard than WordStar does. MicroPro has responded to criticism on this by taking the position that an under-the-fingertips command arrangement is faster than having to reach for function keys and their shifted counterparts. For heavy users who are also excellent touch typists there is merit in this argument. For the majority of us who are less gifted, function keys are in. Later we will cover ways to make better use of them.

Printers of yesteryear also had an influence on program design. The standard printer of only a few years ago did not have the expanded print features of today's models and was almost invariably a 10-pitch machine. WordStar's standard defaults for page offset, column width, and pitch show the influence of these older printer characteristics.

To its credit, MicroPro has followed a path of continuously upgrading and improving its famous offspring. Version 3.3 overcomes several, but by no means all, of WordStar's limitations with an expanded Install program. The new Install program allows you to change numerous start-up parameters by making appropriate menu selections. It also provides for different function key assignments. The new version supports an expanded list of printers as well, although the constant tide of new models makes that a forlorn battle. Many excellent and economical printers are omitted. While the new Install program is a useful improvement, it provides for only limited customizing and is cumbersome to use. Patching gives you access to more functions, and you may also find it ultimately faster and more convenient.

PUTTING YOUR PERSONAL STAMP ON WORDSTAR

Given the limitations imposed by WordStar's roots, you might reasonably contemplate simply putting the old workhorse out to pasture and buying a newer program. You would then have to decide, of course, whether to abandon the substantial learning investment you already have made, and to take on the effort of learning a new program. It could also lead to disappointment unless you happen to find a program which closely meets your needs in stock form. Among leading personal computer software houses, MicroPro has stood almost alone in revealing details of program internals adequate to make customization a practical undertaking. Even they have indicated that this practice will not likely extend to future products or new releases of existing products.

The structure of WordStar itself makes changes easier since the program is largely table driven, meaning that many of its external characteristics can be modified by changes to entries in these tables. Its shortcomings become mostly minor with appropriate customizing. More important, it will then operate in ways better suited to your particular needs and desires. Equally to the point, if your needs change—a good probability in today's dynamic world—WordStar can be adapted to your new requirements.

The modifiable functions of WordStar break down into several major blocks: program defaults, commands assigned to function keys, regular keyboard commands, displays and messages, printed output formatting, and printer interfacing and control. Other useful functions can be changed as well, such as the length of time messages are displayed, the delay before a menu appears, how far a page scrolls right in horizontal scrolling, use of the twenty-fifth screen line, and the choice of characters for numerous display and control functions.

Program defaults affect more than just initial configuration; they also govern many editing, page formatting, and printing functions. For instance, if you usually write multipage manuscripts there is no good reason to stick with a pica-oriented (10 pitch) format—unless you own a paper mill—or to waste time entering numerous preliminary commands at the beginning of every writing or printing session. It is easy to change defaults so that the program comes up in the configuration you use most often, allowing you to begin work immediately.

Printer controls can be set up so that you no longer need to answer the questions in the print menu every time you want to print a file. It's a great timesaver to be able just to press P, enter the name of the file to print, and press Escape. To help you recall what defaults you've set up previously, you can also highlight the appropriate Y's and N's in the menu. That way you won't have to enter an answer just to be sure.

Setting up a program to work with the multitude of printers on the market is a problem for everyone. WordStar in stock form is no exception. More often than not, the main influence on your choice of a printer is not its features, price, or value, but whether it is among the printers listed on the installation menu. Such a limitation is hardly the basis for an optimum selection. Fortunately with WordStar it is not necessary to settle for this. With a reasonably detailed printer instruction manual (which is, among others, a valid factor in your purchase decision) and the proper program patches, it is possible to drive nearly any printer and to obtain maximum performance from it. The chapter on printers will tell you how.

THE TOOLS AND TECHNIQUES OF CUSTOMIZING

Already you have encountered several references to program patching. If you are new to this subject, it may smack suspiciously of the black and arcane arts of programming. Not so. In a roundabout way you are patching when you use the Install program. The difference is that Install selects values based on your inputs, looks up the appropriate addresses, and inserts these values for you. The problem is that your range of choices is limited by what somebody else thought was appropriate. For some seemingly perverse reason, installation programs in general appear to be based on an assumption that you haven't the intelligence or motivation to do it right on your own. Considering how often these programs are themselves obtuse and indefinite in communicating with us, how much time and effort they save in the long run is open to question.

Patching as we will use it is not difficult. It consists first of determining what values are required for a given function and then looking up the address of that function. The Debug program (part of DOS) is then used to access that address in WordStar and to insert the desired values. The main chance for error is inserting a patch in the wrong location. This could cause the program to crash, but more likely it would result in an intermittent bug that could be hard to find. Reasonable care and attention are required. Patching is not recommended activity for the wee hours of a bacchanalian Saturday night.

As you gain experience and take on more ambitious customizing efforts, other tools are also useful. One is a program called SecMod (for sector modification), which is part of the Norton Utilities. Rather than dealing with memory contents, SecMod displays data written on diskettes and provides a fast way of modifying this data directly. (Note: In version 3.0 these capabilities and others have been consolidated in the NU program.) Another helpful technique is dumping WordStar programs to a printer. This allows a more leisurely and broader look at program content.

To assist you in understanding and using these tools effectively, Chapter 2 describes in detail what they are and how to use them. It deals extensively with Debug, which is all you really need unless you wish to embark on an extensive customizing project. Later portions take up other tools and techniques that can be useful additions to your repertoire.

SOME THOUGHTS ON STARTING OUT

How deep you choose to get into customizing WordStar depends on your objectives. You can limit your efforts to purely practical ends or you can expand your horizons to gain insight into program structure and internal operation. In the end, you could find these subjects less formidable and more interesting than you found them at first. Some of you no doubt will find that they hold an intellectual appeal all their own. If you opt for a middle road, you can learn more about how WordStar and your computer work together without becoming embroiled in technical details.

Gains you may make in these directions, however, are added benefits. As said earlier, the main purpose of this book is to help you mold WordStar into a more personalized and therefore more effective writing tool. Some of the material in following chapters is intentionally broad and deep enough for interested readers to learn more than just essentials, but you always have the option of going straight to particulars. In general, the time and effort you spend covering a topic thoroughly will be repaid with improved understanding and better results through a program which is more responsive to your individual style. After all, isn't that what personal computing is all about?

A FEW IMPORTANT NOTES

In following chapters you will often find step-by-step instructions. Data you type on the keyboard as part of these procedures is shown in bold and must be entered as shown. (Except as otherwise noted, you can use either upper or lower case.) Boldface is sometimes also used for important notes. Certain keys pressed in combination, such as <**Ctrl-Alt-Del**>, and other keys such as <**Ret**>, which you may know also as the Enter key, are denoted as illustrated here. Of course you do not include the separating hyphens or the enclosing less-than and greater-than symbols. Control-key shifted keys are denoted by a caret, as in ^**K**, or by the form **Ctrl-K**. The latter is also used for Alt-shifted keys, as in **Alt-J**. Upper-case shifted keys (not to be confused with Caps Lock) are denoted as in **Caps-F1**.

All modifications described in this book have been tested and verified on either version 3.24 or 3.30, and in most cases both. If you are using an earlier release of the program, this does not mean a given change will not work; on the contrary, it usually will. But you should check a listing of the program in the general area where the change is located to be sure that addresses listed herein are correct for your version. Look for the clues provided by table contents, character sequences, and formats described in following chapters. In most cases the overall structure within a given area will not differ from one version to another, but the presence or absence of certain commands or data in a particular version may cause addresses to be shifted higher or lower by a few bytes.

In all cases be sure to use an installed work copy of the program when you are making modifications, and check each change for proper operation. Check your changes on a file you could afford to have damaged or lose if you made a serious error. To protect your investment in previous changes, it is also a good idea to make a fresh working copy of your modified program before embarking on a new round of significant changes. If you should then mess things up beyond recovery, you can resume with your previous copy without having to restart from the beginning. Finally, do not overlook the value of using detailed external labels on your diskettes to distinguish your modified versions.

Although some of these admonitions may seem to have ominous overtones, especially those you find repeated later, their purpose is simply to remind and encourage you to be methodical. With reasonable care, all should be smooth sailing. Happy customizing.

2

GETTING STARTED
THE PROGRAMS AND THE TOOLS

It is possible to customize WordStar a little at a time, picking out the information you need for each modification as you go. If you are not sure at first where you want the process to lead, this is a reasonable way to get started. It can help you decide where you finally want to go, and it's good practice if you're short on experience. But probably you will conclude sooner or later, and correctly, that a more integrated approach produces more cohesive, useful results. The purpose of this chapter is to help build a foundation for that kind of effort.

The initial phases of a WordStar customizing project are not unlike beginning the remodeling of a house. Some knowledge of the structure is required as is an understanding of the tools needed and how they are used. A certain amount of beforehand planning will also be helpful to assure that end results are in keeping with what you envisioned at the start.

WORDSTAR PROGRAMS AND OVERALL STRUCTURE

Although we often refer to it in a singular sense, WordStar consists of not one but three programs, each containing several subsections. The main programs are WS.COM, WSMSGS.OVR, and WSOVLY1.OVR. In contrast to their optional partners, MailMerge and SpellStar (as well as the more recent and expanded spelling checker, CorrectStar, and its companion word counter), these three programs must be present for the system to work properly. Each works with the other two programs and is assigned specific classes of tasks within the operating structure of WordStar as a whole. Knowledge of this structure is useful in becoming familiar with the various functions and where they are located, understanding what routes to your objectives are available, and planning your approach.

WordStar is often described as a heavily overlayed system. That is, its individual programs are composed of numerous smaller modules or segments relating to the functions each performs. These modules have internal names (also referred to as labels) allowing the main program to call them when required. In general, only those program modules currently in use reside in memory at any given time. Other modules are called in from disk as they are needed. Following this, the original modules may be recalled.

This process is called overlaying, since it involves writing a program segment into a portion of memory previously occupied by another segment, in effect laying one over the other. It is among the reasons why WordStar gets along with a relatively small amount of memory, but it also causes frequent and time-consuming disk accesses. This side effect, incidentally, is why using an electronic disk drive in memory is an effective way of speeding up program operation, as will be covered later.

ORGANIZATION OF WS.COM

WS.COM is the heart of WordStar. It contains all the initializing routines for starting the program, the function key and regular keyboard commands, the defaults which establish operating configuration, and the printer control and interface logic. It also calls in various sections of the Messages and Overlay programs as they are needed.

If you use 3.3, it starts out life on your distribution diskette (the original program diskettes supplied by MicroPro) as WSU.COM, the uninstalled version. When you run the install program, default values for numerous operating parameters, including those that you are allowed to select, are written into appropriate locations on your work copy of WordStar. Upon completion of installation, this program becomes WS.COM on your work copy of the program unless you elect to name it otherwise. Earlier versions came with a simpler, less flexible installation program and in some cases were pre-installed for the IBM PC.

Within WS.COM are five functional areas called USER-1 through USER-5. You need not be particularly concerned about these names, as we will deal mostly with individual functions and their addresses. We will refer to them by name at first, since you may already be familiar with two of them, USER-1 and USER-4. Customization notes for these areas were included in manuals for 3.24 and earlier versions, but the information is often cryptic and much of it irrelevant to the usual IBM PC configurations and the MS-DOS/PC-DOS operating system. These notes were dropped from manuals for version 3.3, and MicroPro has indicated that such material is unlikely to be included in the future. This is consistent with trends toward software simplification for new users, but it gives up much flexibility.

Most of USER-1 is devoted to various routines having to do with monitor interface and operation. Many of these either do not apply to the IBM PC or hold little interest for us in a customization sense. Among those that do are the ones dealing with screen height (number of lines), various timing and delay factors for messages, how WordStar is displayed on your monitor screen, choice of default disk drive (not to be confused with the logged-on drive), and how far right the page display moves in horizontal scrolling.

The USER-2 area is a prime candidate for our attentions. It contains all the initial editing and page formatting defaults. Some are selectable with the 3.3 Install program but many are not, and of course, none are in earlier versions. Among these are modifiable parameters for help levels, initial editing toggles, paper size and margins, and the displacements of subscripts and superscripts below and above a line. Also included are initial line spacing, hyphenation criteria, choice of initial characters used to invoke various functions, and default values for print options, including several used by MailMerge.

Keyboard and function key commands are in USER-3. In this area are several tables called keystroke dispatch tables. As you will find when we take up command modifications, these tables are made to order for customizing. All control-letter commands can be two characters long. Function keys can issue any combination of commands up to six bytes in total length. At the end of each table is space for additional entries.

Printer controls are in USER-4 and USER-5. As users of version 3.24 and earlier versions are aware, information presented in the USER-4 notes is adequate for installing simple printers, but absence of details makes the information difficult to use unless you are already knowledgeable. Users of microspacing printers, including many popular daisy-wheel printers, are left mostly in the cold unless theirs is one of the few supported by the Install program. Important controls for these printers are located in USER-5. We will cover all this in the printer chapter.

All of the preceding user areas appear in early sections of WS.COM, beginning around address 0250 and ending before 1000. Except for scattered messages of interest, which are easily found, the remaining bulk of WS.COM consists of program logic code. As you will soon discover when browsing with Debug or examining a printed dump, almost none of it is decipherable. Although expert programmers can unravel parts of it using the Unassemble command in Debug, even this is difficult because of the lack of notes and the very lean and economical nature of assembly language itself. This, however, is of little concern to us; we can accomplish much by working in the user areas described above and detailed in following chapters.

ORGANIZATION OF WSMSGS.OVR AND WSOVLY1.OVR

The messages program, WSMSGS, is quite easy to work with since nearly all of its contents are in plain text which can be read easily with Debug or a similar utility program. (We will get to how to do this shortly.) The program begins with a small block of code which takes care of housekeeping requirements such as identifying the version and handling the pointer table. We need not be concerned with this part of the program.

This is followed by the complete text for each of the menus, beginning with the Opening Menu (known as the No-File Menu in versions prior to 3.3). Next in line is the Main Menu. There are two versions of each, one for 40-column screens and one for 80-column screens. (There are three versions of the Main Menu in 3.3.) You can tell one from another by inspection, and ordinarily you can ignore the former. These menus are followed by Quick, Block, Print, On-Screen, and Help menus; the last also has two versions.

Next is the print dialog text, which is the series of questions about print format you are asked when you initiate the print command. This is followed by the numerous advisory and error messages you see under various operating conditions. It includes those associated with MailMerge. The final and largest block is comprised of the voluminous help texts which are displayed when you select subjects from the Help menu.

The overlay program, WSOVLY1, consists almost entirely of code which implements editing commands and of short messages which accompany these commands. It also includes a printer driver that requires special hardware to operate. Under most circumstances there is little reason for changes to this file. One exception is the status line information which appears in the block beginning at location 4300.

This concludes our brief tour of the WordStar programs. Do not feel you have missed something if a complete picture is not now emblazoned in your mind. It's purpose is to outline groups of modifiable functions and to help you find areas you later may wish to modify but for which specific addresses are not given. Such omissions, incidentally, are restricted to areas which appear in plain text, such as menus and messages, and which are easily found with the tools we will take up next.

THE DEBUG PROGRAM AND HOW TO USE IT

Debug is the name of a utility program provided as part of PC-DOS and MS-DOS. If you are not already familiar with it, a directory listing of DOS will display among the other programs an entry for DEBUG.COM. It is one of our main tools for customizing WordStar.

Although Debug is primarily a diagnostic tool for programmers, and as such contains numerous features we have little need for, it is fast, direct, and handy for displaying and modifying memory contents and for writing such changes to disk. These are exactly the things we need to do, in other words, program patching. It is a way of doing manually, but under your full control and usually faster, what WINSTALL does in version 3.3 of WordStar.

Debug is well documented in your DOS manual, but because of its origin and purpose, not much of the material presented qualifies as light reading. No matter, we will be using only a few of the Debug commands, and these are easy to master with only a little practice.

The commands we will use are as follows: Dump, Enter, Move, Write, and Quit. If you are already versed in using Debug, you can skip the following exercise, although it deals with a useful change. If you are inexperienced, the practice should quickly remove whatever doubts you may have about the ease of using Debug. For this exercise it is assumed that you are using either version 3.24 or 3.3 of WordStar and are using PC-DOS.

On a blank diskette, make a copy of your installed, working version of WordStar using the Diskcopy command. Then copy DEBUG.COM to this same diskette from your DOS diskette using the Copy command. Verify that Debug is present on your new working copy of WordStar by making a directory check. Put a label marked "WordStar test" or something similar on this copy, and insert it in drive A. This completes the preliminaries.

We are now ready to start using Debug, which we will do by actually making a simple modification to WordStar. That was the reason for making a new working copy. If you want an advance look at what you will soon see on your screen, turn now to figure 2-1. This is how the display will look when you finish the exercise described in the numbered steps that follow.

In using Debug commands it is proper to enter only the initial letter, such as D for Dump or E for Enter. You can use either upper or lower case; it doesn't matter. In the following exercise, keyboard entries you must make are shown in boldface. The notation <**Ret**> means to press the Return (Enter) key once. XXXX indicates a number that varies with the version of DOS you are using. (These conventions are used throughout the book.) Proceed as follows:

1. From the A> prompt, type **debug wsovly1.ovr** <**Ret**>. This causes Debug and the WordStar overlay program to load. It is the latter we will modify; note that we must enter its complete name as it appears in the directory, including extension.

2. Upon completion of loading from disk to memory, you will get another prompt that looks something like the cursor but isn't. It's the Debug prompt, a dash, telling you that Debug is waiting for a command. Type **d 4300** <**Ret**>.

3. You will see written to the screen a large block of numbers at left and center, and a small amount of text to the right. The Dump command (d) and the memory address (4300) you entered initiated the display of memory locations starting at the specified address. This will all be explained in more detail shortly, but for the present find line 4350 (left side) and count to the right five pairs of numbers in the large center block. The next entry should be 4F, followed by 4E. These are the memory contents we wish to change.

4. We will now use the Enter command to make the modification. Type **e 4355** <**Ret**>. Debug will respond with XXXX:4355 4F. The value 4F is the memory content at that address.

5. Type **cf** and press the space bar once. *Do not press Return.* Debug will display your entry, skip a space, and display the next memory location, which contains the value 4E. Type **ce** <**Ret**>.

6. We are now ready to write these changes to our WordStar diskette. Type **w** <**Ret**>. Debug responds: Writing XXXX bytes. As you probably have noted by now, Debug executes the current command whenever you press Return and then waits for another by giving you the dash prompt.

7. Now let's dump the same block of memory again to verify that we made the changes as intended. Type **d 4300** <**Ret**>. At locations 4355 and 4356 we should find CF and CE. (Remember, the first location in the row is 0, not 1.) This step is not mandatory, but it is always a good idea to check the changes. An error might not show up immediately in program operation, and it is easier to catch while fresh.

8. Assuming your entries are correct, finish with a Quit command. (If not, you can restore correct values with the same process.) Type **q <Ret>**. This exits Debug and returns you to DOS.

After going through all this, you're probably wondering what the change has accomplished. Load (reboot) your newly customized version of WordStar, and open any file. If Insert is not already on, turn it on. Does the word ON in the status line quickly catch your eye? If you ever insert words when you want to overwrite, or the converse, nothing more needs to be said.

In this exercise we used all the Debug commands we will ordinarily need except the Move command. The few applications we have for it are detailed in later chapters. The Enter command has useful variations you should know about. If you want to examine a location or pass it by without change, just press the space bar without typing an entry. The present value will remain unchanged and you will skip to the next location. If you overshoot and want to back up, enter a hyphen (think of it as minus). If you have entered a long series of bytes and suddenly discover you have made a mistake, it is not necessary to work your way back through laborious corrections if you have not yet issued a Write command. Simply abort the patch by issuing a Quit command. Then reload Debug and the program you are patching, and restart the patch. This should seldom be necessary since most patches will involve only a few bytes, minimizing the chances for error.

There is something else you should know about using the Enter command. If you cross an 8-byte boundary while entering a string of characters, Debug automatically enters a carriage return and line feed. This is no cause for alarm, although it can be startling at first, especially since the line you were on may be only partly filled on your monitor screen. Simply continue entering your string on the new line.

The Dump command is very useful for general scanning or for finding a particular menu or message section. If you alternate between D (or d) and Return keystrokes once you have entered a desired starting address, Debug will take you through successive blocks of memory. Portions of the DOS manual dealing with the above commands are recommended reading.

To amplify certain aspects of the preceding exercise, turn again to figure 2-1, which shows what is displayed on your screen before and after the changes. As you can see, most of the display is occupied by the two memory dumps. The patch itself is quite simple, involving from start to finish only five steps which can be done in far less time than it takes to describe them. We began by loading the Debug and Overlay programs, followed by a memory dump starting at location 4300. At the left side of the ensuing display are addresses expressed in hexadecimal. Those to the left of the colon are presently of no concern; those to the right of it begin with the specified address and continue in 16-byte increments.

In the large central block are actual memory contents, each pair of digits representing one byte expressed in hexadecimal. Each row contains 16 bytes, numbered 0 through F from left to right. For example, the address of the leftmost byte in the top row shown is 4300. That of the rightmost byte in the same row is 430F.

The block at the right side of the screen displays the ASCII character equivalents of bytes displayed in the center block. Values for which there are no equivalents in the set of basic ASCII printing characters are shown as periods. This is generally an advantage, because it eliminates a large quantity of visual clutter when you are looking for text in English.

If the entire subject of hexadecimal and ASCII characters seems rather dark and mysterious to you, Appendix A is recommended reading as well as a useful reference. Actually, it is not necessary to develop more than a nodding acquaintance with these characters. You will still be able to accomplish a lot. But the subject is not as formidable as it may seem, and your level of computer literacy will leap upward if you persevere.

OTHER HELPFUL UTILITY PROGRAMS

A growing number of what could be termed general purpose disk utilities are available. They allow direct manipulation of data on diskettes and can be useful additions to your customization tool kit. Although Debug can do everything you need to do, a good disk utility program can make some tasks, such as modifying messages, easier and faster. These utilities can also reveal useful and sometimes surprising facts about how programs and data are organized on your diskettes.

Among the most popular of these generally inexpensive programs are the Norton Utilities. Although you may seldom have need for all, two members of the set are especially helpful. They are DiskLook and SecMod (version 2.0). Both are fast and convenient to use. In version 3.0 these programs have lost their identities to the new NU program, and some functions have been abridged. If you have the earlier version, you may find it more useful.

DiskLook makes it easy to see how the files on a diskette are organized as well as providing other useful and interesting data about file formats, sector assignments, and the like. If you have ever noticed that the disk drive you use for WordStar text files seems to grunt and groan a lot, and that it gets worse as you manipulate text, DiskLook can quickly show you why.

As you create, revise, and save, disk sector assignments (made by DOS, not WordStar) become increasingly random. In a short time your files can be fragmented and scattered all over the diskette, causing large and frequent excursions of the disk head as it reads and writes. The result is slower accesses and increased wear and tear on your drive, a good thing to minimize by occasionally copying your files to a new diskette using the Copy *.* command. This puts the file sectors back in physical sequence, at least until we do more editing and saving. It is also good backup practice which we all tend to ignore—sometimes to our subsequent dismay.

SecMod, a contraction of sector modification, allows you to modify the data on a diskette directly and simply. Unlike Debug, which works best in hexadecimal, SecMod allows you to tab to the ASCII portion of its display and type changes in English. This is a great time saver and avoids much counting of bytes—and potential errors—when you are modifying WordStar menus or message texts. Unfortunately, it does not ignore high-order bits which WordStar uses to create highlighted characters. The ASCII display of these characters in SecMod is not directly readable, and you are better off using Debug for highlighted portions of menus and messages.

USING THE WORDSTAR 3.3 PATCHER

Your first reaction may be, "What patcher?" It is undocumented in the WordStar manual, but nevertheless it exists in WINSTALL, the installation program. Although CP/M versions of WordStar have long included a patcher, release of 3.3 marked the first time one was available in PC-DOS versions. It follows a generalized installation utility concept now implemented by MicroPro, emphasizing broader selections on installation menus but playing down customization capabilities.

The patcher is accessible from the installation menu, which you reach after lengthy preliminaries. At the bottom of this menu you are prompted to "Enter the letter of your choice (A/B/C/D/E/X)." Not included is the key which unlocks the door to the patcher, a + (plus sign). When you enter the plus sign, an on-screen response indicates that you are entering the custom modification routine. An advantage of the patcher is that with appropriate prefixes you can make entries in ASCII, hexadecimal, or decimal. You can also access an area directly by memory address or indirectly by label, if you know the label. Neither addresses nor labels are given. (However, all addresses and many labels are listed for patchable functions in this book.) Since the patcher steps through and displays successive memory addresses and contents at the same time, it is most helpful when entering long strings or modifying a table. Not so good is that it confines access to limited areas of WS.COM and provides no access to the messages and overlay programs.

A serious liability is all the overhead you must put up with to use the patcher. By the time you wade through Winstall's extended preliminaries, lengthy on-screen explanations that would be better left to the manual, and many yes/no pauses, you could in most cases have long since loaded Debug, made your patch, and quit. Ironically, the patcher itself is sometimes too terse and can leave you wondering where you are or what to do next.

DUMPING PROGRAM FILES TO A PRINTER

Any time you make more than a few modifications, a printed program dump will prove to be a useful tool. To begin, it can give you a much better perspective on program organization than you can get by scanning with Debug or SecMod one screen at a time. True, it will not read like a book, but you might be surprised how much you can learn from it. You will also find it a handy medium for making and saving notes. Finally, a dump printed at the end of a project quickly and conveniently documents your modifications.

Although a specialized utility program for printing file dumps is the most convenient, programs for this purpose are not common. You can produce a printout using nothing more than Debug and the DOS echo printing command, Ctrl-PrtSc. Load Debug and the program you wish to dump, and use the Dump command to find the area you wish to print. Then activate the printer and issue the print command. Enter D and the starting address (if you enter just D with no address, it will start at the beginning of the file); the printer will then print the following eight lines, stopping with the Debug prompt. From that point simply enter D again, and the printer will continue with the next block. This method is not especially fast, but it is usable. Printing the first 1,000 locations in WS.COM will provide a reference to most of what you need.

A simple but effective dump utility program written in Basic is listed in Appendix B. Consisting of less than 70 lines of code, it will produce dumps not only of your WordStar programs but any other as well. The printed output of this program is similar in appearance to the display you get with Debug's Dump command. This is a help, since you often use them together. It overcomes a shortcoming of Debug by adding numbers across the top of each block to identify individual byte locations. It will run on nearly any printer without special setups.

TECHNIQUES FOR GETTING STARTED

We have now covered the basic tools and techniques you need for making WordStar a more personalized and effective writing tool. If you are already experienced at customizing, your main interest probably lies in finding ways to add further enhancements. Following chapters should provide a quantity of new grist. If you are less experienced, the remainder of this chapter presents a few ideas that may prove helpful—not only in getting started but in putting together an overall approach.

Before turning to these topics, we will repeat a bit of advice given earlier: Always make your modifications to a working copy of WordStar—not your main working copy, but a second copy. That way if you make a serious error it may be necessary to restart with a fresh copy, but your regular working copy and original WordStar diskette will stay intact. As you add modifications, backup this copy frequently. You can then recover gracefully if calamity strikes, without having to re-input all your previous changes. Remember, you are in effect creating a new master, so give it all the care a master deserves.

Keep in mind also that you should always make your modifications to an installed version of the program. Depending on the operations you select, the Install program otherwise may overwrite some of your previous entries and cause much head scratching until you figure out what happened.

Being aware of possibilities is an essential part of developing a good approach. It is recommended that you skim through the following chapters to gain insight to what can be done. Some material may not be of interest, and some may not seem to apply to your needs at this point. No matter, you will then know about it and can decide later how or if it fits.

Consider the kinds of writing you do and your own individual writing habits. Do you write in spurts, with frequent breaks calling for quick saves and a return to where you stopped? Do you revise a lot—make numerous block moves or deletes—often use temporary files to create or move sections in or out of your main text? Do you use a lot of formatting commands? Do you have difficulty remembering some commands (not necessarily those you use infrequently), or do you make certain errors repeatedly?

These considerations and more have direct bearing and influence on how you can customize the program for maximum benefit. Problems with certain commands or repetitive errors, for example, may suggest not ineptness but function key assignments or keyboard commands that are inappropriate for you as an individual. It might be helpful to make an informal list with two headings: I wish the program did . . . I wish it didn't.

Such a list will not only pinpoint specifics but may also reveal one or more patterns which can cue you in a particular direction. You might also find helpful the chapter on Getting It All Together—but with reservations. Examples shown there are drawn largely from the personal experiences and requirements of others. A different way of doing things might prove better for you.

You may wonder why so much emphasis is placed on a planned, integrated approach. The reason is that we are dealing with what advanced designers and human factors experts refer to as ergonomics, the techniques of fitting machines and technology to the characteristics and needs of humans. These processes are based on proven concepts, but for economic reasons the reality is that industry adapts them to mass markets, not individuals.

We can use the same techniques, however, to reach practical and useful objectives: to enhance our personal creativity and productivity by making the automated tools we use do our bidding with as little conscious effort on our parts as possible. To whatever degree we succeed, we free ourselves to concentrate on our real work.

Figure 2-1. Example Of Program Dump And Patch Using Debug

```
A>debug wsovly1.ovr
-d 4300
22BD:4300  9A 01 05 05 00 00 00 00-A0 8D 0A 00 00 E9 16 0D   ........ ....i..
22BD:4310  E9 81 07 C3 6A 00 14 00-18 00 1D 00 1F 00 22 00   i..Cj.........".
22BD:4320  26 00 2C 00 34 00 00 00-38 00 50 41 47 45 5C 00   &.,.4...8.PAGE\.
22BD:4330  20 4C 49 4E 45 5C 00 46-43 3D 00 20 46 4C 3D 00    LINE\.FC=. FL=.
22BD:4340  20 43 4F 4C 5C 00 4D 41-52 5C 52 45 4C 00 49 4E    COL\.MAR\REL.IN
22BD:4350  53 45 52 54 5C[4F 4E]00-64 65 63 69 6D 61 6C 00   SERT\ON.decimal.
22BD:4360  4C 49 4E 45 5C 53 50 41-43 49 4E 47 5C 00 00 00   LINE\SPACING\...
22BD:4370  00 00 00 00 00 00 00 00-00 00 00 00 00 00 5A 00   ..............Z.
-e 4355
22BD:4355  4F.cf   4E.ce
-w
Writing A100 bytes
-d 4300
22BD:4300  9A 01 05 05 00 00 00 00-A0 8D 0A 00 00 E9 16 0D   ........ ....i..
22BD:4310  E9 81 07 C3 6A 00 14 00-18 00 1D 00 1F 00 22 00   i..Cj.........".
22BD:4320  26 00 2C 00 34 00 00 00-38 00 50 41 47 45 5C 00   &.,.4...8.PAGE\.
22BD:4330  20 4C 49 4E 45 5C 00 46-43 3D 00 20 46 4C 3D 00    LINE\.FC=. FL=.
22BD:4340  20 43 4F 4C 5C 00 4D 41-52 5C 52 45 4C 00 49 4E    COL\.MAR\REL.IN
22BD:4350  53 45 52 54 5C[CF CE]00-64 65 63 69 6D 61 6C 00   SERT\ON.decimal.
22BD:4360  4C 49 4E 45 5C 53 50 41-43 49 4E 47 5C 00 00 00   LINE\SPACING\...
22BD:4370  00 00 00 00 00 00 00 00-00 00 00 00 00 00 5A 00   ..............Z.
-q
```

Note: Refer to text for discussion.

3

MODIFYING FUNCTION KEYS AND CURSOR CONTROLS

Until WordStar version 3.3 was released, modifying function keys was at best difficult due to lack of information on memory locations and formats. In the main you were stuck with existing key assignments, whether they met your requirements or not. Information on making modifications has gradually leaked out, but most often the changes described also involve specific key assignments. Unless these happen to fit your needs, you aren't much further ahead. Moreover, trying to glean from these modifications a set of general rules to fit all situations can become an exercise in frustration.

This will be rectified here by explanations of basic command formats and the requirements for making key assignments so that you can make any choice you wish. Also described are the various cursor control keys, the insert and delete keys, and the backspace key. Included is a way to modify the effect of the delete key so that it deletes the character above the cursor, instead of to its left, and to change backspace key action so that it erases characters as you backspace. We will also cover how you can make a modest expansion in the number of function keys available and how to create shifted cursor-pad and function keys.

With version 3.3 the installation program lets you change function key assignments, but as mentioned earlier this can be a slow process—especially if you want to experiment with the feel and utility of various combinations. Once you have mastered the technique of using Debug, you will probably find it faster and more convenient. Debug is a necessity, of course, if you are using an earlier version of the program.

The advent of keyboard enhancers capable of redefining nearly any key has in some ways obviated the need for patching WordStar to reassign keys and change commands. However, they do add their own overhead in the form of added expense, additional time to load whenever you start up, and a slight although not obvious reduction in command execution speed. Actually there often is good reason to use keyboard enhancers and directly redefined keys in combination, capitalizing on the advantages of each. How to use keyboard enhancers with WordStar is covered in Chapter 7.

FUNCTION KEY COMMAND STRUCTURE

Space for function key assignments is located in WS.COM in a table labeled FUNTAB. In standard IBM PC form, this table contains space for a total of 20 entries. These include the ten function keys on the left side of the PC keyboard, the eight cursor control keys on the numeric keypad, and the insert and delete keys below. The arrangement is the same for most PC work-alikes having a similar keyboard layout and using MS-DOS, but there can be variations. The Texas Instruments PC is a case in point. While not touted as an IBM compatible machine, it uses an MS-DOS version of WordStar which is generically standard but provides for twelve function keys rather than ten. The function key table is slightly different in structure and is in a different location within WS.COM—an example, by the way, of in-house customizing by MicroPro.

Unlike the other WordStar command tables, where each entry contains an internal address which ties it to a specific program function, entries in the function key table contain a data byte which relates a given entry to a specific key on the keyboard. This data byte contains a keyboard scan code which is unique for each key. Whenever you press a key that is listed in this table, WS.COM looks up the scan code entry for that key, reads the command characters entered there, and executes the commands as if you had pressed their individual keys directly.

The format for entries in the function key table is fixed and contains a total of nine bytes for each entry, the first two relating to scan codes. Normally you need be concerned with only the seven which follow those: one byte specifying the number of command bytes and up to six command bytes.

Interesting and useful changes can be accomplished by manipulating scan codes, but the procedures are more involved. They are described later in the section on advanced techniques.

Since space for up to six command bytes is available, you can combine instructions to be executed by a single function key. For example, you could have up to six single-character commands or up to three two-character commands, or any other combination totaling six characters. (Shifted keys, such as Ctrl-Q, count as one character.)

MAKING FUNCTION KEY CHANGES USING DEBUG

While function key structures may seem complex, the basic process of making changes is simple. First, determine what commands you wish to assign to a particular function key. Always use the control-character and capital-letter representations of these commands. Let's say, for example, that you wish to use F7 to position the cursor at the left side of the screen (^QS). Look up the address for F7 in table 3-1 at the end of this chapter. Next you need to convert ^QS to its hexadecimal equivalent, using table A-2 in Appendix A. You will find that the value for ^Q is 11 and the value for S is 53. This is a total of two bytes, so your entry for length is now also determined. Since we have used only two bytes of the six available, the remaining bytes should be filled with asterisks, or hex 2A.

You will probably find it helpful and more error-free to jot your inputs down on paper, especially if you are going to make several function key changes at one time. The following format is suggested:

Key	Address	Length	Cmnd: ^Q	S	* to fill field
F7	06A6	02	11	53	2A 2A 2A 2A

You are now ready to enter inputs into WS.COM to make a change. The general procedure is as follows. (See Chapter 2 if you need more details on using Debug.)

1. Load Debug and WS.COM: A>debug ws.com
2. Select starting address (XXXX) using the E command: -e XXXX
3. Enter desired bytes starting with length byte, ending string with <Ret>: xx.nn xx.nn xx.nn etc.
4. Finish with Write and Quit commands.

If you are not sure of the process, let's go through an exercise. We will assign to F1 (or any function key of your choice if you substitute the appropriate starting address) a command which saves your current file to disk and returns you to the end of the file. It is very useful for periodic saves as you are writing or to capture what you have entered if you are called away briefly but intend to continue. The required commands are ^KS and ^QC. Again we jot down the required information.

Key	Address	Length	Cmnd: ^K	S	^Q	C	* to fill field	
F1	0670	04	0B	53	11	43	2A	2A

We now are ready to make the actual patch. In the following example, your required entries are shown in boldface. Variable responses made by Debug are shown as X's. After you enter the E command and type the first byte, remember to press the space bar once after an entry to step to the next entry. Do not press return until you have made the final entry in the string. If you make a mistake, simply quit and restart. (In this exercise an on-screen CR-LF inserted by Debug will occur while you are entering data, as described in Chapter 2, but it will not affect the patch.)

A>**debug ws.com <Ret>**
-e 0670 <Ret>
XXXX:0670 XX.**04** XX.**0b** XX.**53** XX.**11** XX.**43** XX.**2a** XX.**2a** **<Ret>**
-w <Ret>
Writing XXXX bytes
-q <Ret>
A>

When you reload WordStar, the new command will be in effect. As a practical matter, it is not actually necessary to enter the asterisk bytes since the length byte specifies to the program how many following bytes are to be taken as commands. However, none of the unused bytes can be zeroes (00), for that could signal a false end to the table. It is also good practice to make sure that unused bytes are asterisks to prevent confusion later. Before issuing the Quit command, you might also wish to double-check the patch by entering a Dump command and the starting address.

Under most circumstances you will probably have no need to modify the arrow keys or the home, end, page up, page down, and insert keys. The delete key is another matter, and a useful change also involving the left arrow key but not changing its action is detailed in the next section. For the sake of completeness, locations and data entries for all these keys are included in tables at the end of this chapter. The formats are identical with those of the function keys.

CHANGING ACTION OF THE DELETE AND BACKSPACE KEYS

In most programs the delete key deletes the character above the cursor and the backspace key is destructive, erasing characters as you backspace. WordStar, as you doubtless know, is different. Although the backspace key is destructive when you respond to a question prompt (such as FILE NAME?) it does not operate this way when you need it most often—as in text editing. Then it merely trails along duplicating the action of the left arrow key. The delete key, on the other hand, acts like a destructive backspace.

The following patch is for users who prefer more typical key responses. Addresses are correct for all PC versions of the program.

```
A>debug ws.com <Ret>
-e 0499 <Ret>
XXXX:0499 08.13 <Ret>      (unties Bkspc from ^S)
-e 0529 <Ret>
XXXX:0529 7F.08 <Ret>      (creates destructive Bkspc)
-e 053a <Ret>
XXXX:053A 7F.08 <Ret>      (enables ^Q-Bksp)
-e 06e6 <Ret>
XXXX:06E6 08.13 <Ret>      (puts ^S on left arrow key)
-e 071c <Ret>
XXXX:071C 7F.07 <Ret>      (puts ^G on Del key)
-w <Ret>
Writing XXXX bytes
-q <Ret>
A>
```

When this patch is installed, pressing the Del key will then delete the character above the cursor. When held down, the key will continue deleting characters to the right. The backspace key becomes destructive, deleting characters to the left, one with each strike or continuously when held down. Thus, the action of these modified keys is pleasingly complementary. As a result of these changes, the standard delete-to-beginning-of-line command (^Q-Del) is disabled. In versions prior to 3.3 it didn't work anyway. In its place is a new command, ^Q-Backspace, which does work and conceptually is more consistent with a destructive backspace. This patch also unties the backspace key from the left arrow key, which other patches may not do.

Again, if Debug responses to your <Ret> commands differ from specified values while making the patch, quit without writing to disk and investigate. Also quit and restart if you make a mistake. As always, it is a good idea to reload WordStar and exercise the command immediately after making the patch to check results.

FUNCTION KEY ASSIGNMENT CONSIDERATIONS

Given that you can assign up to six bytes of commands to any function key, the natural tendency is to get as much mileage as possible by filling them all up. This is not necessarily a good thing to do. It is better to consider first your writing and editing habits. After all, saving one or two keystrokes on a command you use constantly will save you more effort in the long run than some elaborate combination you seldom use.

If you do a lot of word and phrase smithing after a first draft is complete, putting commands such as Delete Word Right (^T) and Delete To End Of Line (^QY) on function keys may make sense. It may also be helpful in another way: reaching for a function key is a more deliberate action than tapping keys directly under the fingertips. The slight mental gear changing involved might often save you from flushing important material. If you also frequently use various block moves to shift whole sentences and paragraphs around, then it makes sense to include block beginning and end markers and the most often used block move commands. If you use WordStar for different writing applications, it could be useful to create more than one working version of the program, each having different key assignments. A certain amount of restraint is advised here, however, as making smooth operating transitions from one version to another then might prove difficult.

The point is that WordStar function key resources are limited on the PC, so it pays to give assignments careful thought. Unfortunately, the internal structure of WS.COM makes it very difficult to add shifted function keys, although it can be done in a limited way. If you need several more function keys, the most practical answer is to use a keyboard enhancer as described in later chapters. To stimulate your thinking on function key assignments, some practical examples are given in Chapter 8.

ADVANCED TECHNIQUES FOR EXPERIENCED CUSTOMIZERS

Commonly expressed among users is a desire that WordStar would provide for shifted function and cursor control keys. Being able to use Ctrl, Alt, and upper-case shifts would quadruple the number of function keys available. Cursor control key functions could likewise be expanded but only doubled since the IBM PC allows only for Ctrl-key shifts on these keys.

The main hindrance to adding shifted function keys to WordStar is not program logic but lack of table space. While other command dispatch tables contain space for additional entries, the function key table contains space for only 20 entries, all of which are used. Another shorter table, used for special merge-print commands, follows immediately, leaving no intervening space that could be used.

Old hands at customizing WordStar might respond that tables can be moved to reallocate expansion space. This is ordinarily true, but the function key table presents a special problem. Following the merge-print dispatch table is a short pointer table which must be updated to contain new starting addresses whenever command tables are moved. It contains entries for the No-File (now called Opening) command table, the editing command table, and the merge-print command table. Unfortunately, there is no entry for the function key table. Apparently a direct form of addressing was used when this table was added to accommodate the PC's function keys, in effect shutting the door to moving it.

There is, however, a roundabout way of approaching the problem which produces a small gain in available space. By moving the merge-print command table to expansion space left at the end of the editing command table, we can gain enough usable space at the end of the function key table to add two more commands. Another approach that might be used by those familiar with assembly language is to find an appropriate place at which to insert a patch linking the function key table with a larger expansion area, but such an effort would go well beyond ordinary customizing techniques.

If you elect to move the merge-print command table, a patch that does this for either 3.24 or 3.3 is as follows.

```
A>debug ws.com <Ret>
-m 0724 0734 065d <Ret>             (moves merge-print table)
-e 0739 <Ret>
XXXX:0739 24.5d 07.06 <Ret>         (updates pointer table)
-w <Ret>
Writing XXXX bytes
-q <Ret>
A>
```

The preceding patch moves 17 bytes including the merge-print command table and its terminating zero byte to location 065D, which falls near the end of expansion space provided in the editing command table. MicroPro's notes state that the function key table needs two zero bytes to terminate it, but one byte appears to work if it is the first byte in a function key command field. Thus we gain a total of 18 bytes to work with, or enough for two complete commands. The second step in the patch updates the pointer table so that the program knows where to find the moved merge-print table. If you decide to try another location, remember that multibyte addresses are expressed in memory with the least-significant byte first.

USING SHIFTED FUNCTION KEY AND CURSOR COMMANDS

Having created a small amount of added working space in the function key command table with the procedure just described, we can now consider adding commands. Since we have no additional keys, adding commands can be done only by using the shift functions, Caps, Ctrl, and Alt.

The length of a complete command is nine bytes arranged in the format shown below:

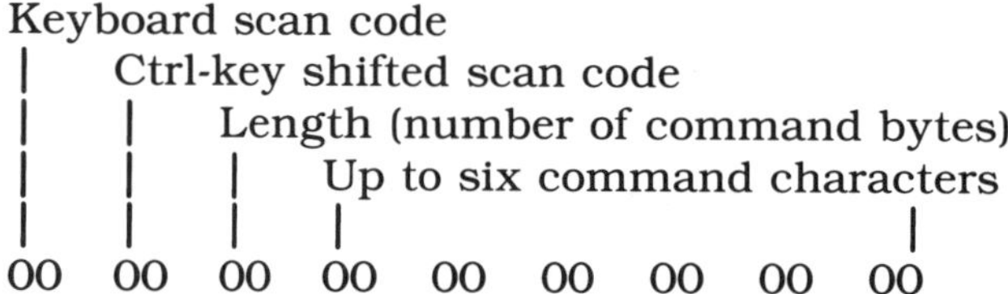

The PC keyboard generates a unique one-byte scan code for each key. WS.COM reads this code and looks for it in the function key table. If it finds the code, it interprets the length byte and associated command characters, and executes the command by going to the editing command table.

Apparently MicroPro at one time had in mind allowing the control key to be pressed along with a function key, as is done for the regular keyboard commands. However, there appears to have been a subsequent change of mind. At any rate, the Ctrl-key-shifted scan code byte is unused, and equivalent Ctrl-shifted function key commands do not work.

This does not mean, however, that you cannot use shifted function key commands—only that you must put the appropriate scan code in the first byte. By doing so you can use the full range of valid shifted function keys as well as control-shifted cursor pad keys. The scan codes for these keys are listed in table 3-2.

Some interesting and useful pairs of "naturalized" combinations can thus be installed. (Addresses given are usable with both 3.24 and 3.3, but only if you have moved the merge-print command table as described.) For example, the following patches make Control-left-arrow and Control-right-arrow move the cursor a word left (^ A) and a word right (^ F), respectively.

Addr: 0722	73	00	01	01	2A	2A	2A	2A	2A
Addr: 072B	74	00	01	06	2A	2A	2A	2A	2A

Alternatively, the next patch produces Control-Home and Control-End commands which take you to beginning-of-file and end-of-file (^ QR and ^ QC) respectively, freeing the usual F9 and F10 assignments for other uses.

Addr: 0722	77	00	02	11	52	2A	2A	2A	2A
Addr: 072B	75	00	02	11	43	2A	2A	2A	2A

A challenge is left for enterprising and resourceful readers to find a fail-proof way of creating space for a full range of shifted function and cursor-pad keys. This would require approximately 400 bytes. A limitation on using existing patch areas is that the install program may overwrite them whenever it is run. If you find a suitable location, remember to include space for one or more zero bytes to terminate the table. Without such, the table search routine could run amok.

Table 3-1. Function Key And Cursor Pad Key Locations
(Applies to versions 3.24 and 3.3)

Format:

```
Length (number of command bytes)
|      Up to six command characters
|      |                          |
00    00    00    00    00    00    00
```

Label: FUNTAB

Key	*Addr*	*WS-Equiv*	*Key*	*Addr*	*WS-Equiv*
F 1	0670		Home	06CA	^QS^QE
F 2	0679		↑	06D3	^E
F 3	0682	varies	Pg Up	06DC	^R
F 4	068B		←	06E5	Bkspc
F 5	0694	with	→	06EE	^D
F 6	069D		End	06F7	^QX^QD
F 7	06A6	version	↓	0700	^X
F 8	06AF		Pg Dn	0709	^C
F 9	06B8		Ins	0712	^V
F10	06C1		Del	071B	^G

USE THESE ADDRESSES FOR NORMAL MODIFICATIONS

Table 3-2. IBM PC Function-Key And Cursor-Pad Scan Codes

		← shifted keys →		
Key	*Norm*	*Caps*	*Ctrl*	*Alt*
F 1	3B	54	5E	68
F 2	3C	55	5F	69
F 3	3D	56	60	6A
F 4	3E	57	61	6B
F 5	3F	58	62	6C
F 6	40	59	63	6D
F 7	41	5A	64	6E
F 8	42	5B	65	6F
F 9	43	5C	66	70
F10	44	5D	67	71
Home	47	X	77	X
↑	48	X	X	X
Pg Up	49	X	84	X
←	4B	X	73	X
→	4D	X	73	X
End	4F	X	75	X
↓	50	X	X	X
Pg Dn	51	X	76	X
Ins	52	X	X	X
Del	53	X	(System Reset)	

Note: Values in hexadecimal; X = invalid combination

Table 3-3. Function Key And Cursor-Pad Key Locations

(Applies to versions 3.24 and 3.3)

Format:

```
Keyboard scan code
|    Ctrl-key shifted scan code (see text)
|    |    Length (number of command bytes)
|    |    |    Up to six command characters
|    |    |    |                        |
00   00   00   00   00   00   00   00   00
```

Key	*Addr*	*Key*	*Addr*
F 1	066E	Home	06C8
F 2	0677	↑	06D1
F 3	0680	Pg Up	06DA
F 4	0689	←	06E3
F 5	0692	→	06EC
F 6	069B	End	06F5
F 7	06A4	↓	07FE
F 8	06AD	Pg Dn	0707
F 9	06B6	Ins	0710
F10	06BF	Del	0719

DO NOT USE THESE ADDRESSED FOR NORMAL MODIFICATIONS

(Refer to table 3-1)

4

MODIFYING THE EDITING AND FILE COMMANDS

This chapter covers the numerous editing and file commands used in WordStar. In addition it covers commands used in merge-printing and the selection of control characters used in various editing and file operations. Also included are the basic cursor control commands.

Some of these have already been discussed in the preceding chapter in connection with cursor-pad and function keys. However, as described there, these keys merely duplicate and simplify the keying of commands that are part of the repertoire presented here. The basic commands, their formats and format variations, selection of command characters, and how they can be modified are defined and explained in this chapter.

WordStar file and editing commands are organized into several tables called keystroke dispatch tables. Included are tables for opening menu commands (formerly the no-file menu), editing commands, and certain merge-print commands. Following these are a pointer table, the details of which are covered later in this chapter, and an area for defining the special control characters mentioned above.

BASIC COMMAND AND TABLE STRUCTURES

Each entry in the command dispatch tables consists of four bytes: two bytes for command characters (sometimes only one is used) and two bytes for an internal program address or offset value of the associated program logic. This address entry provides the link between command characters and a given function, such as "set left margin." The command itself, in this instance ^OL, could just as easily be any other unused character or two-character combination. A restriction on this is that a two-character command cannot use as its first character one used as a single-character command. However, any command that is presently one character can be expanded to two.

There is an advantage to two-character commands in that if you realize you have made a mistake after typing the first character, you can escape by merely pressing the space bar. However, a two-character command is clearly slower to use than a single-character command. The trade-off you must make, therefore, is speed versus the safety factor of being able to escape from the command after the first character is typed.

Although there are slight variations in the way certain classes of commands are implemented, their general format is shown in the following illustration. Normally you do not need to be concerned with the internal address except to be sure that it is not altered.

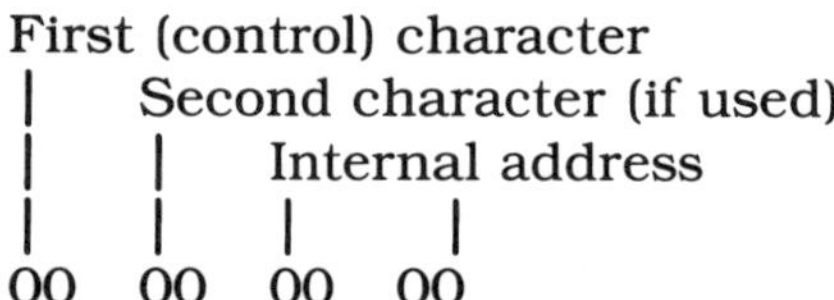

The first character must be a control character; that is, one having a hexadecimal value between 01 and 1F. This is for the program to distinguish between command characters and text characters when you are entering text or editing. The program assumes that the character following is also a command character unless the second byte in the table entry is zero. The second may be any character, but a letter must be in upper case or its control-shifted equivalent (a lower-case letter actually typed as the second keystroke is converted internally to upper case before the table search).

Each of the tables contains space at its end for additional command entries. A zero in the first-character position terminates the table.

Program logic for these tables, unlike that for function-key tables, does not recognize keyboard scan codes. Instead, it recognizes only the basic 127 characters of the ASCII character set, which precludes the use of Alt-key-shifted characters as commands. You can still use such characters if you wish, but a keyboard enhancer program is required.

OPENING (NO-FILE) MENU COMMANDS

Opening menu commands are shown in table 4-1. (Numbered tables refer to tables in this book, not to program tables.) The program table contains entries for each command letter appearing on the opening menu display, as well as for two that do not: ^Z and ^W for scrolling the directory.

Program logic already expects an initial command character when you are at the opening menu. This is why it is not necessary to type a control-key prefix from the keyboard. All commands are a single character, meaning that the second byte is always zero in the standard implementation. (By entering a value for an upper-case letter or other character of your choice, you can make these two-character commands if you wish.) Only keys listed in the table are active at this point in program operation. If you press the key for a character not listed, the program scans the table to look for it and, not finding it, does nothing except wait for another keystroke. This is as close to fail-safe operation as you can get.

Entries added at the end of the table may only use existing functions since there is no corresponding program logic to implement new functions. You can use this space to assign alternate command characters to an existing command. An example is to add a command so that you could use either D or some other unused letter to open a document file. If you add alternates, the address portion of the original command (i.e., the two bytes at the end) must be carefully copied to the address section of its alternate.

In general, adding alternate commands is not recommended practice; it tends to negate the mistake-proof qualities of having active the minimum number of keys needed to cover all commands. If you need to make a change, it would be better to simply modify the main command.

EDITING COMMANDS

The editing command dispatch table is activated whenever you open a file, either new or old. Details of table entries are shown in table 4-2. It begins with entries for four of the five help menus which are displayed when you type the prefix for an editing command: ^J, ^K, ^O, or ^Q (unless you have suppressed menu display by selecting a help level of 0 or 1). You normally will not want to change these. The printing help routine accessed by the ^P prefix is located in an overlay file.

These initial commands are followed by the normal editing, cursor control, and scrolling commands, as well as others on the quick menu. Next are text block and place markers, followed by block move, copy, delete, and column mode commands. Remaining commands on the block menu are next in line. These are succeeded by commands from the on-screen and help menus. You will find in some cases that there are alternate commands, not all of them meaningful on the IBM PC but present as holdovers from versions for other equipment.

Note that some of these commands have references to related special characters. These special characters are discussed below. Normally they should agree with associated editing commands; if you change one, you should also change the other.

MERGE-PRINT COMMANDS

A few commands related to printing with the MailMerge option are listed in table 4-3. Others relating to selection of dot command characters are included in the chapter on setting up defaults. Most of the dot commands themselves are not readily accessible. Again, if you change a related edit command, it would be wise to change here as well to prevent confusion.

TABLE POINTERS AND SPECIAL CHARACTERS

As mentioned previously, the opening-menu, editing, and merge-print command tables have pointers to tell the program where these tables begin. If you move any of these tables to rearrange available space, a procedure not recommended unless you have a fair amount of experience, the pointers must be updated to contain the new starting addresses. Pointers consist of two-byte entries for the table address. A multibyte address is always entered with the least-significant byte first. For example, a starting address of 0430 is entered as 30 04. Details for these and the following special character entries are given in table 4-4.

There are six control characters which are applicable to operations involving responses to prompts ending in a question mark, such as "File Name?" or "Find?". An example is ^P, meaning in this application to take the next character literally, and enabling the use of control characters in a search argument. Although it is not mandatory, normally you will want these characters to agree with their editing counterparts.

The final two entries are for the interrupt (^U) and error release (Esc) characters. The interrupt character must agree with the corresponding entry in the editing command table or the editor will not work right. The error release character may be changed to any other of your choice. Unless you have a strong reason for change, however, it is probably best to leave these as they are. A change would require updating numerous messages.

HINTS AND PRECAUTIONS

Many useful changes to WordStar file and editing commands are possible, but because of limitations imposed by command structure and program logic most fall in the category of fine tuning. If you wish to make large-scale changes, such as adding a complete series of Alt-shifted commands, the most practical way of doing that is with a keyboard enhancer.

Before you use any part of available expansion space, always be sure that WS.COM has been installed for your system configuration. Then check the expansion space with Debug. In some cases the Install program uses portions of this space and would overwrite anything you had previously entered there. Remember that usage of this space, if any, may vary from one installed configuration to another, depending on options you select.

If you use expansion space to create additional (alternate) commands, be sure to copy carefully the two-byte internal address of the original command to the corresponding space in the new one. Be aware that these internal addresses may change from one WordStar release to another.

TECHNICAL NOTES ON TABLE OPERATIONS

The following are brief notes for readers interested in understanding how the tables are scanned and commands are interpreted and implemented during program operation. What tables are scanned and the scanning sequence depend on where you are in the program.

At the opening menu, only the opening (no-file) command dispatch table is scanned. When a keystroke is entered, the program scans the table to find the corresponding character. If it finds the character, the program reads the associated address entry and branches to the instructions located there. If, for example, a letter D is pressed, the program requests a file name, loads the file from disk, calls in appropriate sections from the Overlay file, and activates the function-key and editing command dispatch tables. If a letter P is pressed, the program branches to the the printing routines. When the entry is a letter M (assuming the MailMerge program is present), both the printing routines and the merge-print command dispatch table are activated.

When editing, both the function-key and editing command tables are searched. Each key on the IBM PC keyboard has a unique one-byte scan code, and the program first looks for these codes in the function key table. When it finds a match, the program reads the associated command characters and looks for these characters in the editing command dispatch table. At this point, the sequence of events becomes the same as if you had entered the command characters directly. The editing command table is searched to find matching entries, and as directed by the related internal address entry, the program branches to appropriate instructions for execution of the command or commands.

The pointer table is worth special mention. Since WordStar includes provisions to accommodate reorganizing or moving of command tables for the opening menu, editing, and merge-printing functions, the program may need assistance in finding these tables. Before a table is searched, the pointer table is scanned to find the starting address of the table to be searched. In effect, the pointer table acts like the directory in the lobby of an office building. The pointer table itself cannot be moved except through reassembling the complete program, since its internal addresses are set at assembly time. This, of course, would require facilities and source data not available in the field.

Table 4-1. Opening Menu (No-File) Commands

Format:

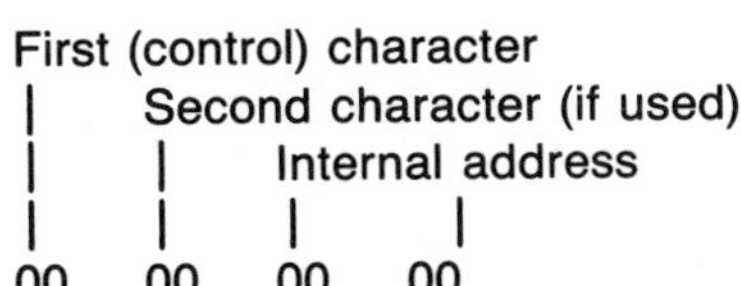

Label: NOFTAB

Addr	*Std-Val*	*Equiv*	*Function*
0430	04 00	^D	Open document file
0434	0E 00	^N	Open non-document file
0438	08 00	^H	Set help level
043C	18 00	^X	Exit to system (DOS)
0440	10 00	^P	Print a file
0444	0D 00	^M	Initiate Merge-Print
0448	19 00	^Y	Delete a file
044C	06 00	^F	File directory on-off
0450	1A 00	^Z	Scroll directory up
0454	17 00	^W	Scroll directory down
0458	0C 00	^L	Change logged disk drive
045C	12 00	^R	Run a program
0460	0F 00	^O	Copy a file
0464	05 00	^E	Rename a file
0468	16 00	^V	(Not implemented)
046C	13 00	^S	Run SpellStar/CorrectStar
0470	00 00	—	Expansion space
0474	00 00	—	Expansion space
0478	00 00	—	Expansion space
047C	00 00	—	Expansion space
0480	00		Terminates table if all expansion space used

Table 4-2. Editing Commands

Format:

```
First (control) character
|     Second character (if used)
|     |     Internal address
|     |     |     |
00    00    00    00
```

Label: VTAB

Addr	*Std-Val*	*Equiv*	*Function*	*Notes*
0481	11 FF	^Q	Prefix for Quick menu	(1)
0485	0B FF	^K	Prefix for Block menu	(1)
0489	0F FF	^O	Prefix for On-screen menu	(1)
048D	0A FF	^J	Prefix for Help menu	(1)
0491	0A 08	^J^H	Set help level	
0495	13 00	^S	Cursor left character	
0499	08 00	Bkspc	Alternate for above	
049D	04 00	^D	Cursor right character	(2)
04A1	01 00	^A	Cursor left word	
04A5	06 00	^F	Cursor right word	
04A9	18 00	^X	Cursor down line	
04AD	05 00	^E	Cursor up line	
04B1	11 13	^Q^S	Cursor left side of screen	
04B5	11 04	^Q^D	Cursor right end-of-line	
04B9	11 18	^Q^X	Cursor bottom of screen	
04BD	11 05	^Q^E	Cursor top of screen	
04C1	11 42	^QB	Cursor to block begin	(3)
04C5	11 4B	^QK	Cursor to block end	(3)
04C9	11 50	^QP	Cursor to previous position	(3)
04CD	11 56	^QV	Cursor to last find/replace	(3)
04D1	11 30	^Q0	Cursor to marker zero	(3)
04D5	11 31	^Q1	Cursor to marker one	(3)
04D9	11 32	^Q2	Cursor to marker two	(3)
04DD	11 33	^Q3	Cursor to marker three	(3)
04E1	11 34	^Q4	Cursor to marker four	(3)
04E5	11 35	^Q5	Cursor to marker five	(3)
04E9	11 36	^Q6	Cursor to marker six	(3)
04ED	11 37	^Q7	Cursor to marker seven	(3)
04F1	11 38	^Q8	Cursor to marker eight	(3)
04F5	11 39	^Q9	Cursor to marker nine	(3)
04F9	11 12	^Q^R	Cursor to beginning-of-file	
04FD	11 03	^Q^C	Cursor to end-of-file	

Table 4-2. Editing Commands (Continued)

Addr	*Std-Val*	*Equiv*	*Function*	*Notes*
0501	11 06	^Q^F	Find string	
0505	11 01	^Q^A	Find and replace	
0509	11 0C	^Q^L	Find misspelling	
050D	0C 00	^L	Find and replace again	
0511	11 17	^Q^W	Start scrolling down	
0515	11 1A	^Q^Z	Start scrolling up	
0519	1A 00	^Z	Scroll up a line	
051D	17 00	^W	Scroll down a line	
0521	12 00	^R	Page down	
0525	03 00	^C	Page up	
0529	7F 00	Del	Delete character left	
052D	1F 00	^_	Alternate to above	
0531	07 00	^G	Delete character at cursor	
0535	19 00	^Y	Delete entire line	
0539	11 7F	^QDel	Delete to beginning of line	
053D	11 1F	^Q^_	Alternate to above	
0541	11 19	^Q^Y	Delete to end-of-line	
0545	14 00	^T	Delete word right	
0549	16 00	^V	Insert on-off	
054D	02 00	^B	Reform paragraph	
0551	11 11	^Q^Q	Repeat next command	
0555	0E 00	^N	Insert blank line	
0559	09 00	^I	Tab right	
055D	0D 00	^M	Carriage return, line feed	
0561	10 00	^P	Print menu prefix	(4)
0565	0B 08	^K^H	Hide/display marked text	
0569	0B 42	^KB	Mark block beginning	(5)
056D	0B 4B	^KK	Mark block end	(5)
0571	0B 30	^K0	Set/hide marker zero	(5)
0575	0B 31	^K1	Set/hide marker one	(5)
0579	0B 32	^K2	Set/hide marker two	(5)
057D	0B 33	^K3	Set/hide marker three	(5)
0581	0B 34	^K4	Set/hide marker four	(5)
0585	0B 35	^K5	Set/hide marker five	(5)
0589	0B 36	^K6	Set/hide marker six	(5)
058D	0B 37	^K7	Set/hide marker seven	(5)
0591	0B 38	^K8	Set/hide marker eight	(5)
0595	0B 39	^K9	Set/hide marker nine	(5)
0599	0B 16	^K^V	Move marked text	
059D	0B 03	^K^C	Copy marked text	

Table 4-2. Editing Commands (Continued)

Addr	Std-Val	Equiv	Function	Notes
05A1	0B 19	^K^Y	Delete marked text	
05A5	0B 0E	^K^N	Column block mode on-off	
05A9	0B 1A	^K^Z	(blank)	
05AD	15 00	^U	Interrupt	(6)
05B1	0B 18	^K^X	Save file and exit	
05B5	0B 04	^K^D	Save, done editing	
05B9	0B 13	^K^S	Save and resume editing	
05BD	0B 11	^K^Q	Abandon edit	
05C1	0B 12	^K^R	Read file into text	
05C5	0B 17	^K^W	Write marked block to file	
05C9	0B 0A	^K^J	Delete a file	
05CD	0B 06	^K^F	File directory on-off	
05D1	0B 10	^K^P	Print a file	
05D5	0B 0C	^K^L	Change logged disk drive	
05D9	0B 0F	^K^O	Copy a file	
05DD	0B 05	^K^E	Rename a file	
05E1	0F 0C	^O^L	Set left margin	
05E5	0F 12	^O^R	Set right margin	
05E9	0F 09	^O^I	Set tab stop	
05ED	0F 0E	^O^N	Clear tab stops	
05F1	0F 06	^O^F	Set margins/tabs from text	
05F5	0F 17	^O^W	Word wrap on-off	
05F9	0F 0A	^O^J	Justification on-off	
05FD	0F 16	^O^V	Variable tabs on-off	
0601	0F 04	^O^D	Hide/display print controls	
0605	0F 14	^O^T	Ruler line display on-off	
0609	0F 10	^O^P	Page-break display on-off	
060D	0F 05	^O^E	Soft hyphens on-off	
0611	0F 08	^O^H	Hyphen-help on-off	
0615	0F 07	^O^G	Paragraph tab	
0619	0F 18	^O^X	Margin release	
061D	0F 03	^O^C	Center line	
0621	0F 13	^O^S	Set line spacing	
0625	0A 04	^J^D	Explain dot commands	
0629	0A 13	^J^S	Explain status line	
062D	0A 06	^J^F	Explain right-side flags	
0631	0A 10	^J^P	Explain place markers	
0635	0A 02	^J^B	Explain paragraph reform	
0639	0A 0D	^J^M	Explain margins and tabs	
063D	0A 09	^J^I	Display index of commands	

Table 4-2. Editing Commands (Continued)

Addr	Std-Val	Equiv	Function	Notes
0641	0A 16	^J^V	Explain moving text	
0645	0A 12	^J^R	Explain ruler line	
0649	00 00	—	Not used	
064D	00 00	—	Expansion space	
0651	00 00	—	Expansion space	
0655	00 00	—	Expansion space	
0659	00 00	—	Expansion space	
065D	00 00	—	Expansion space	
0661	00 00	—	Expansion space	
0665	00 00	—	Expansion space	
0669	00 00	—	Expansion space	
066D	00		Terminates table if all expansion space used	

Notes:

(1) Changes not recommended.
(2) See delete character at 073C (Table 4-4).
(3) Uses internal markers 1-4 and 6-15, respectively.
(4) See print control prefix at 073E (Table 4-4).
(5) Sets internal markers 1, 2, 6-15, respectively.
(6) See interrupt character at 0742 (Table 4-4).

Table 4-3. Merge-Print Commands

Format: Same as edit commands **Label**: FPTAB

Addr	Std-Val	Equiv	Function
0724	10 00	^P	Pause-resume printing
0728	1A 00	^Z	Scroll directory up
072C	17 00	^W	Scroll directory down
0730	16 00	^V	(no external function)
0734	00		Terminates table

Table 4-4. Pointers And Special Characters

Addr	*Std-Val*	*Equiv*	*Function*	*Notes*
0735	30 04	—	Pointer to opening (no-file) command table	(1)
0737	81 04	—	Pointer to edit command table	(1)
0739	24 07	—	Pointer to merge-print table	(1)
073B	00		Reserved for expansion	
073C	13	^S	Delete character left	(2)
073D	04	^D	Cursor to right character	(2)
073E	10	^P	Take next character literally	(3)
073F	06	^F	Turn directory on if off	(2)
0741	17	^W	Scroll directory down	(2)
0742	15	^U	Interrupt character	(4)
0743	1B	Esc	Error release character	(2)

Notes:

(1) Standard value is starting address of table, least significant byte first. (30 04 reads as 0430, etc.)

(2) Characters used in responding to prompts for "FILE NAME?", "FIND?", etc. Nearly any character will work, but all should be consistent with corresponding editing commands.

(3) Permits entry of control characters in search arguments.

(4) Must agree with corresponding entry in editing command table.

5

CHANGING ON-SCREEN DISPLAYS AND MESSAGES

As the window to your work and the pipeline for operating feedback, WordStar's visual characteristics are second only to keyboard operations in their influence on your relationship with the program. Although attributes of the monitor itself are also involved, the way that menus, messages, and text are displayed on-screen has an important bearing on ease of operation, how many mistakes you make, and your level of overall productivity. If you often spend hours at a time writing or editing, attention to display modes can influence both the quantity and quality of your output and how you feel at the end of a long session.

Much of this is subjective. Researchers have yet to reach general agreement on visual standards for monitor hardware, and consensus on how to optimize software in a visual sense seems a long way off. A practical approach you can take, which ultimately may prove to be the correct solution anyway, is to deal with all this on a personal level, choosing whatever works best for you as an individual.

The familiar appearance of WordStar on the screen of your monitor is not the only way it can be displayed. Nor is it necessary to live with menu contents or messages which are not appropriate to the way you have set up the program. All these can be changed to make them more suitable to your configuration and methods of operation.

You might find, for example, that a fully lighted screen with solid black characters is not only easier on the eyes but more closely simulates a printed page. This can shorten the path between ideas and words on paper, and it can help alleviate the frequent feeling that somehow the printed output looks vastly different from what you saw on your screen. On the other hand, you may be happy with nothing more elaborate than a few message changes or a means of making block-marked text more prominent. The bottom line is that this is fertile ground for personalized enhancements.

ALTERING THE SCREEN DISPLAY MODE

The normal WordStar screen display on monitors capable of character highlighting is with menu headings and entered text in bright (highlighted) characters. Other portions of menus and the top-of-screen status line display in normal (dim) intensity. Marked blocks of text are changed from bright to dim when the end-of-block marker is entered.

On the IBM PC and its work-alikes, how these items are displayed is controlled by three WS.COM internal functions labeled IVON, IVOFF, and IBMATT. The IV in the first two labels stands for Intensified Video. In spite of what its name might suggest, IVON controls the display of normally non-highlighted areas. The IVOFF function controls normally highlighted areas, while the IBMATT function controls initial screen color. The latter on a monochrome monitor, whether IBM or composite, is obviously limited to either black or the color of the screen phosphor, but on a color monitor, you can select any of the many colors available. (In this chapter the term monochrome is used in a generic sense unless otherwise noted.)

What follows now is a brief technical explanation of how the on-screen display is controlled. It is centered on the IBM color/graphics adapter but applies also to systems using the monochrome adapter except for portions referring to color. If you prefer not to get involved with the details, you can go directly to figure 5-2 and related text where suggested alternate display modes are listed and discussed.

The above display control functions are each represented in memory by what IBM refers to as an attribute byte. The term attribute denotes the display characteristics. Among these are normal (dim), reverse, highlighted (intensified), and blinking characters. These attribute bytes also control foreground and background colors—black or white (or green, amber, etc.) on monochrome monitors and the full palette of colors on color monitors.

The data entries at these memory locations are in hexadecimal, but the individual bits of their binary equivalents, acting as on-off switches (one for on, zero for off), actually do the controlling. As shown in figure 5-1, each of the eight binary bits controls a different attribute.

Figure 5-1. Typical Attribute Bytes For Displays In Monochrome

Bit pos in attribute byte 7 6 5 4 3 2 1 0	Screen Color (background)	Character Color (foreground)	Hexadecimal Equivalent
0 0 0 0 0 1 1 1	Black	White	07
0 1 1 1 0 0 0 0	White	Black	70
0 0 0 0 1 1 1 1	Black	White (H)	0F
1 0 0 0 0 1 1 1	Black	White (Bl)	87
1 0 0 0 1 1 1 1	Black	White (H,Bl)	8F
Bl R G B I R G B	← Display functions controlled		

Bits 0-2 control the foreground, bit 3 is the intensity bit which turns highlighting on or off, bits 4-6 control the background, and bit 7 turns character blinking on or off. The foreground and background control bits, labeled R, G, and B for red, green, and blue, control corresponding electron guns in the typical color display tube. As you might expect, these bits manipulate screen and character colors when you are using a color monitor. For black or white on both color and monochrome monitors, they are either all off (black) or all on (white).

By setting foreground color along with the intensity and blink control bits, you can achieve varied effects in the way characters are displayed. Some of the effects possible are indicated in figure 5-1 by notations H for highlighting and Bl for blinking. The required bit patterns are derived from appropriate hexadecimal inputs at IVON, IVOFF, and IBMATT. (Values for other combinations can be found with conversion data in Appendix A.)

Figure 5-1 does not show all possible combinations of the attribute byte, and not all are useful with WordStar. It is doubtful, for example, that you would want to use blinking characters since you cannot use them selectively. You should keep in mind that the attributes you choose apply across the board to whatever function is involved. That is, if you wanted dim menu headings and entered the appropriate byte for IVOFF, your entered text would also be dim—not necessarily a good choice.

The memory addresses for these functions, their standard hexadecimal values, and two useful alternates are shown in figure 5-2.

Figure 5-2. Some Useful Combinations For WordStar Displays

Address: Function:	0284 IVON	028B IVOFF	02D5 IMBATT	Result (Applies to both 3.24 and 3.3)
Normal	07	0F	07	Dim menus, status; bright text
Alt-1	07	70	70	Black characters on white screen
Alt-2	70	0F	07	Normally dim items in reverse

The first alternate is a good choice if you prefer a bright screen with black characters and do not have a monitor which allows switching directly to inverse video. The prominent scan lines with a color/graphics monitor adapter are much less noticeable in this mode, since they do not go through the displayed characters. (There are the lines that make characters look like the IBM logo.) Also, displayed text appears more nearly as it would on a printed page, which you may consider an advantage. However, you do lose the benefit of two levels of character brightness.

The second alternate is also good on standard monitors, particularly if you prefer block-marked text to stand out more than it does in the usual dim characters. It has the added advantage that spaces are marked as well, which is a help in column block moves. Normally highlighted characters are not affected. Those that are normally dim appear in black against a reversed, dim background. Contrast and brightness controls work normally, so you can adjust the relative brightness of highlighted and dim areas as usual.

Method two is even better if you have a monitor with switchable inverse video capability. With the monitor thus switched, items which are dim in standard configuration appear as bright characters on dark backgrounds, while text appears in black on a fully lighted screen. This provides the closest possible simulation of a printed page with readily available hardware. There are other advantages as well. Messages stand out clearly, appearing as bright characters against surrounding black patches. Block-marked text really pops onto the screen, and hyphens at end-of-line word breaks and other soft hyphens appear prominently in reverse. You also have the option, of course, of switching back to the normal dark screen for variety.

The on-screen appearance of this arrangement is shown in figure 5-3. Note that the ruler line appears as a black band across the top of the screen, providing desirable visual separation between ruler and status lines and your text below. (This is most noticeable when there are lines of text directly below the ruler line, as is usually the case.) With the standard display, block-marked text is not always distinct unless you are careful about setting contrast and brightness controls on your monitor. It makes little difference with this arrangement; text blocks are in black with the text they contain shown in reverse.

Figure 5-3 Reverse Screen With Modified Display Attributes

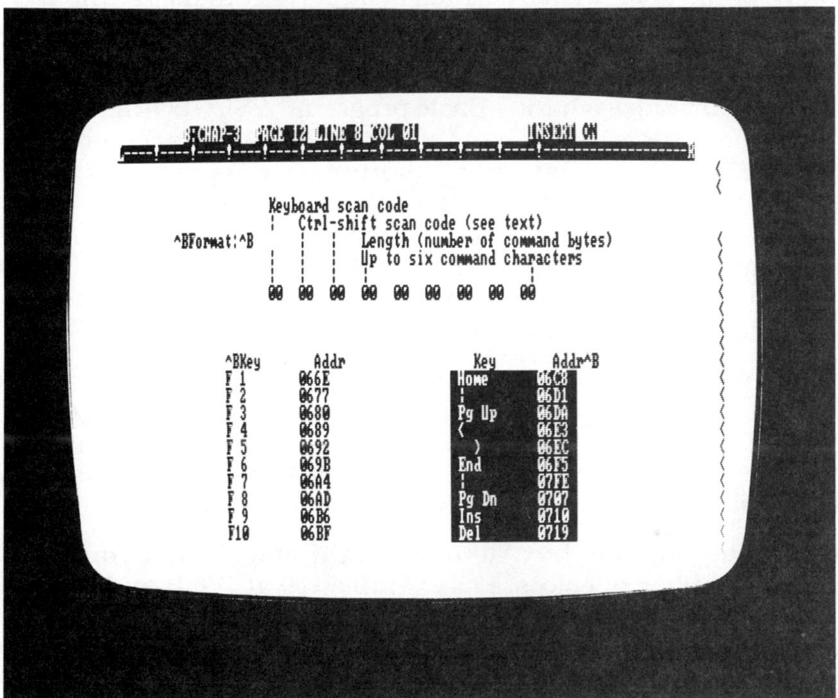

Couple all this with an amber screen and you have a combination that is very easy on the eyes. The amber screen, for no apparent reason beyond wider availability of green, is catching on slowly in North America while becoming a standard in Europe. Although experts do not yet agree on which produces less eye fatigue, amber is closer to the peak of human spectral response than green, and amber usually causes less after-image effects (the effect that occurs when you look away). Human psychological response to color introduces yet another variable, so in the end, it still may boil down to personal preference. But if you have an opportunity to try this setup do so, especially with a fully lighted screen. As a fringe benefit you may find the golden-sunrise effect more inspiring to the flow of words than staring into the video equivalent of a black hole.

CHANGING COLORS ON COLOR MONITORS

For heavy users of word processing systems, color monitors at their present stage of development are at best a mixed blessing. Even with an IBM color/graphics adapter, which does not have the resolution of the monochrome adapter and its display, images on a composite monochrome monitor (available from a host of manufacturers) are sharper than those on a color monitor. A color monitor, on the other hand, has the obvious advantage of full color display which is important to users who work also with graphics-oriented applications—not to mention writers who indulge in an occasional game.

WordStar 3.3 includes a handy Basic program, WSCOLOR.BAS, featuring an in-color menu for selecting color combinations. It does required patching of IVON and IVOFF automatically. Unfortunately, users of earlier versions are left with manual patching as the only means of changing colors. The technique is the same as for monochrome, except that RGB and intensity bits are manipulated to vary the colors displayed. Thus, it is possible to have the screen in one color, non-highlighted characters in a second color, and highlighted areas in a third color.

Unless you want a reversed screen (IBMATT = 70), proper selection of the attribute bytes for IVON and IVOFF will also control the screen color, since these values are moved to IBMATT by the program as required. Some representative values are shown in figure 5-4. Fundamentals discussed earlier in connection with figure 5-1 apply here also.

By entering appropriate hex values at IVON and IVOFF, you can obtain many combinations of colors. For example, 19 at IVON and 1E at IVOFF yields light blue messages and yellow text against a blue background. Likewise, values of 6A at IVON and 6E at IVOFF would produce light green messages and yellow text on a brown backgound. The points to remember are as follows:

1. Colors are determined by which attribute bits are turned on, both in the background (bits 4-6) and the foreground (bits 0-2).
2. Red, green, and blue are turned on by the single corresponding bits. Red and green together result in brown. Green and blue result in cyan. Red and blue result in magenta. Red, green, and blue result in white.
3. Turning on the intensity bit results in foreground colors which are lighter variations of the corresponding basic colors. The exception is brown, which becomes yellow.

Figure 5-4. Example Color Combinations For Color Monitors

Bit pos in attribute byte 7 6 5 4 3 2 1 0	Screen Color (background)	Character Color (foreground)	Hexadecimal Equivalent
0 0 0 1 1 0 0 1	Blue	Lt Blue	19
0 0 0 1 1 1 1 0	Blue	Yellow	1E
0 0 1 0 1 0 1 0	Green	Lt Green	2A
0 0 1 1 1 0 1 1	Cyan	Lt Cyan	3B
0 1 1 0 1 1 1 0	Brown	Yellow	6E
0 1 1 0 1 0 1 0	Brown	Lt Green	6A
Bl R G B I R G B	← Display functions controlled		

To assist in determining the hexadecimal numbers required to produce the bit pattern appropriate to your color selections, a chart is included in Appendix A. If you are not familiar with working in binary, read the accompanying discussion of bit numbering conventions. If you simply ignore bit-position numbers and match up the required bit patterns beginning with the rightmost bit, you should have no difficulty.

Opting for colored backgrounds with 3.24 and earlier versions results in untidy menus and messages, possibly because MicroPro did not anticipate using color this way. They could be cleaned up, but it would require long, tedious patching. (In version 3.3 this has already been done, which may be a good reason for upgrading if you are a color aficionado.) Therefore, you may wish to leave the background dark. To do this, set the background RGB bits to zero. Yellow characters, for example, would thus require an input of hex 0E, while light blue characters would require a hex value of 09, and light green a 0A. Make these inputs at IVON or IVOFF, depending on whether you want to change menu or text character colors.

MODIFYING WORDSTAR MESSAGES AND MENUS

By the time you get well into a customizing project, you will probably find that some of the standard messages are no longer appropriate or that they and menu contents could be improved. Small touches like highlighting INSERT ON or the default values displayed in menus can pay off in greater ease and speed of program usage. Individually such changes may make only slight differences, but collectively they can add up to substantial gains.

Messages are among the easier things in WordStar to modify. Text for messages and menus is written in the program in plain language and appears as such at the right side of the screen when using Debug. Most messages are in WSMSGS.OVR, although some are in WS.COM and WSOVLY1.OVR. If you make extensive changes a printed dump will prove handy, since it provides a much broader view than you can get from a single screen at a time.

In WordStar, characters are highlighted by setting the eighth or high-order bit (a discussion of high-order bits and how they are used is included in Chapter 11). This can be done by adding a value of 80h to the hex value of the normal character. The value of a letter D, for instance, becomes C4 instead of 44. A much easier way is to refer to table A-2 in Appendix A, where you will find required conversion information shown at the head of each column except the first two, which do not apply.

As with other modifications, using the Enter command (E) in Debug is effective for making changes once you have found the right area. You can also use the SecMod (or NU) program from the Norton Utilities for several kinds of changes, subject to limitations described in Chapter 2. SecMod is handy and quite fast, but remember to press F9 as the final step, which writes your changes to disk.

Whatever scheme you use, it is wise to consider beforehand just what you wish to accomplish in the way of changes. Check how the unmodified message is displayed on-screen. It may be centered in some larger space, you may want to make it shorter or longer if space is available, or you might want to shift it right or left. Count characters and spaces and lay out a simple diagram before proceeding with actual modifications; you will be much less likely to lose your place or spill over into adjacent areas. Then examine the patch area with Debug or SecMod to verify that everything will fit properly.

To illustrate the utility of message changes and how to make them, let's consider the print dialog that appears on-screen whenever you initiate the Print command (P). This is the series of prompts that allow you to specify whether you want disk output, use of form feeds, pause for paper change, etc. Those that can be answered yes or no each have a default position, but unless you have only a single printing setup and use it all the time, you may not always remember how the defaults are set. You can eliminate this problem, and thereby do away with having to enter an answer to each prompt, by highlighting the Y or N in the display for each one. (Before doing this you should decide on and enter the defaults you want to use as described in Chapter 6.)

The print dialog is in the WSMSGS.OVR file. In version 3.3 it starts in the block beginning at address 3300; in version 3.24 it begins at 2F80. When you load Debug and this file and dump the appropriate address, you will see the dialog text in the ASCII section of the display. It extends through several 128-byte blocks, so you may have to use successive D commands to reach the portion you want to change.

Using the Disk Output prompt in 3.3 as an example, examine the contents beginning at 33DD. You will find the characters **(Y/N)** having hex values 28 59 2F 4E 29. If the default selected was No, we will highlight the N. To provide further emphasis, we can delete the enclosing parentheses and use the freed area to allow insertion of highlighted spaces flanking the letter N. Thus, the new entry beginning at 33DD would be Y-slash-space-N-space or, in hex, values of 59 2F AO CE AO. You can use this same technique for the remaining prompts as well as other message changes.

If you select an alternate screen display mode permanently, especially the second of those described earlier, you may wish to do some cleaning up of the menus. Since items like menu headings are set off distinctly by contrasting backgrounds, flanking dashes and arrows are not necessary. In fact, you may feel that they only add visual clutter. Finding and altering the menus is not difficult. They appear early in WSMSGS.OVR, beginning at about location 0300 and ending around 2160. Remember that some menus have 40-column versions that are not used. If you make a change and it does not show up when you reload, you probably made it on the wrong menu.

HINTS AND PRECAUTIONS

When making changes, keep in mind whether you are working with highlighted or non-highlighted characters and whether you are in a normal or reversed display area. Values entered for even non-printing characters such as spaces are important. The hex value of a highlighted space, for example, is AO rather than 20. If you confuse the two, you can end up with black spaces where you wanted white and vice versa. Chances still are good that you will make an error or two, but this is not a serious problem. Any errors will show up promptly when you reload WordStar, and at worst, you will have to go back for corrections.

Finally, be cautious about altering any unusual characters preceding or following a message. In some cases these are delimiters or index characters used by the program to identify messages. Changing them can cause strange and unintended effects. Even this, however, need not be cause for panic if it happens, since it is easy to restore original data with another patch. You should have a printed dump of the patch area on hand before starting the modification so you can back up to the original if necessary.

Display changes when coordinated with other modifications add greatly to the ease of using your custom version of WordStar. They are among the most visually dramatic of the many changes you can make, and at the least, they'll impress your friends and associates with your expertise.

6

CHANGING START-UP AND OPERATING DEFAULTS

Although the main theme of this book is on meeting your needs as an individual, you probably have at least one motivation in common with other users of word processors—to save time and effort. In that vein, it is more than a petty annoyance to be forced through a series of preliminary setup commands every time you start the program. Inevitably it seems, flashes of creativity strike at odd times—most often when the PC is cold and seldom when the Opening Menu sits quietly awaiting our commands. Those fleeting moments of inspiration are too valuable to let their prompt apprehension be circumvented by mere program mechanics.

Fortunately, it is not necessary to put up with such roadblocks. Almost all of WordStar's start-up and operating parameters can be changed to meet your requirements, reducing overhead and speeding up operations. You can select page size and margin parameters, specify the initial state of editing toggles, select numerous control and display characters, control hyphenation criteria, rename WordStar program files, and predefine yes/no answers to questions in the print initiation dialog.

Several of these defaults became more accessible with the release of version 3.3 and their inclusion in the installation menu, but there are important omissions. Users of earlier versions will find this chapter even more useful. For convenience, defaults are presented and discussed in order of their appearance in memory. For some functions no discussion is needed, and they appear only in the listings at the end of the chapter.

CHANGING START-UP DEFAULTS

Start-up defaults are those which establish an operating condition or parameter when the program is initiated from a cold start or reboot. Many are simply on-off toggles; an entry of 00 means off and FF means on (with certain exceptions noted later). Others require actual values, such as for margins and other page sizing parameters. Most are accessible by command, but the purpose of changing defaults is to set up the program the way you most often use it, avoiding the need to issue these commands repeatedly.

Help Level. Four levels are available. A setting of 03 provides maximum help; the main menu is displayed at all times when editing. A setting of 02 suppresses the main menu and provides more screen space for displaying text. A setting of 01 suppresses the individual menus which normally appear (after a selectable delay) when the prefix of an editing command is entered; only advisory messages appear. A setting of 00 suppresses all help.

The entry following the help level controls display of a message, FOR MAXIMUM HELP TYPE ^JH3, which appears at the beginning of an edit session if the selected help level is 1 or 2. It is normally suppressed (FF), but can be enabled (00) if you wish. (The roles of FF and 00 here are in a sense reversed, "on" in this application meaning to suppress.)

Page Format. This is a series of 25 bytes that establishes page parameters for length, top and bottom margins, heading and footing margins, number of lines per page, the number of printed characters per inch, and the printed page offset. These parameters, except the last two, affect the page-break display, and all affect the printed page format. Standard default values are based on paper size of 8-½ X 11 inches and line spacing of 6 lines per inch. Top and bottom margins, heading margin, and footing margin are all expressed in numbers of lines. Default values for most page parameters can be overridden by entering appropriate dot commands in your text file, but only microspacing printers respond to those involving incremental motion.

Line height is another way of expressing lines-per-inch; it is stated in 1/48-inch increments. The standard default value of 08 is derived from 48/6, where 6 is the number of lines per inch for single-spaced printing. Similarly, the value needed for 3 lines per inch (double space) would result from 48/3, which is a line height of 16 or, in hex, a value of 10.

Paper length is expressed two ways: first in lines per page and then in 48ths of an inch. For example, a paper length of 11 inches at 6 lines per inch is 66, or hex 42. The following two-byte entry is line height times paper length, or 8 X 66 which is 528, or 210 hex. (Remember that the format in memory is least-significant-byte first, or 10 02.) Similarly, for legal-size paper length of 14 inches, the length is expressed as 84 (i.e., 6 X 14) or 54 hex. The value in 48ths would be 672 (i.e., line height times paper length, or 8 X 84) or 2A0 hex, entered as A0 02.

The top margin is expressed like paper length: first the number of lines, then its equivalent in 48ths. Thus we have the normal value of 3 or ½ inch, followed by line height times number of lines (8 X 3) or 24, which is 18 hex. Again, this is entered as two bytes in reverse order, or 18 00. Heading margins, bottom margins, and footing margins are all calculated and entered the same way.

Character width values are based on 120ths of an inch. The standard pitch of 10 characters per inch (cpi) therefore is 120/10, equal to 12, or 0C in hex. The alternate pitch of 12 cpi is 120/12, equal to 10, or a hex value of 0A. (If you were not already aware of it, you now know the source of those seemingly strange dot commands such as .CW 12 for 10 cpi and .LH 16 for double line spacing.) If you want to substitute an alternate pitch of 15 cpi, the equivalent is 120/15, or 8 in decimal and hex. If you use 15 cpi, you should also be aware that the maximum number of columns selectable by default (76) limits you to a printed column width of just over five inches (76/15) unless you reset the right margin and accept the need for constant horizontal scrolling to see your text. This is feasible for short blocks, but beyond that there is little joy in it.

Page offset is the number of columns to the right the print head moves from its home position before starting a line of printing. Most printers allow some latitude in physical positioning of paper, and you may find that cut sheets feed more smoothly at one position than another. By adjusting page offset value you can match up the first print column with the smoothest feeding position. Top and bottom margin defaults may also need adjustment, since rolling a sheet in far enough to reach the paper bail effectively lengthens the top margin and shortens the bottom margin.

Since all the preceding parameters can be altered with dot commands in text, there normally is little reason to use anything other than standard single spacing (6 lines per inch) as a baseline for page format parameters. (Remember, however, that some dot commands, such as .LH and .CW, work only on a microspacing printer.) If you are using version 3.3 your selections can be made from the Install program, avoiding the need for calculations and conversions of large numbers from decimal to hexadecimal. This is one place where the installation program offers an advantage over Debug.

Margin Settings. The default settings establish the initial left and right margin columns. Normally they are set at columns 1 and 65, producing column widths of 6-½ inches at 10 pitch but less than 5-½ inches at 12 pitch. If you commonly use 12 pitch, you will probably want to reset the right margin default for a wider column.

The left margin default is set to the desired column number minus one. That is, for a left margin in column 5 set the default to 04. Valid values are from zero to the right margin column number minus three.

The right margin default is also the desired column number minus one. The range of valid values is from 2 to the screen width minus four. For a standard 80-column screen this limits the right-most setting to column 76. At a pitch of 12 this produces a printed column width of about 6-3/8 inches. Allowing for the minus one, the relevant hex value is 4B. Larger values can be entered, but the program automatically truncates them. (After start-up you can reset the right margin with ^OR to a maximum of 240.) This default is also used in merge printing.

Subscript/Superscript Roll. On microspacing printers this default governs the amount the carriage rolls the paper up or down to print a subscript or superscript. It is expressed in 48ths and is normally set to 03, or half a line. Larger values will displace characters further, smaller values less. Accessed by a .SR dot command.

INITIAL EDITING DEFAULTS

On-Off Toggles. These entries control start-up states of various editing functions such as word-wrap, justification, ruler-line, page-break displays, and so on. Values are 00 for off and FF for on, and no other values should be used. They are used only in document mode; in non-document mode all are cleared by the program.

There are two page-break toggles. If on, the first causes page-break data to be collected internally while editing. If set to zero, information is not collected and associated high-order bits in the text file are not set. When set to zero, it in effect disables the second toggle (the normal page-break display). It is not accessible by keyboard command. The second toggle controls the actual display or non-display of page breaks and current page number in the status line at the top of the screen. Usually you will not need to be concerned about either of these toggles.

Line Spacing. Normally set to 1 (single space). Set to 2 for double space, etc. This affects both on-screen display and printed output. If you want more than single-spaced output, it is better with microspacing printers to use an appropriate .LH command at the beginning of a text file. This both conserves screen space and produces the desired output line spacing.

Block Mode. With normal setting (00), the program starts in standard block mode. If set to FF, it comes up in column block mode.

File Opening Mode. This toggle controls the opening mode when WordStar is invoked from the DOS prompt with an accompanying file name: document mode if 00; non-document mode if FF. If you normally use an autoexec batch file to start, the setting is irrelevant.

Decimal Point Character. Use this to define the character that ends the right-alignment action when using decimal tab stops. It is normally a period, but you may enter another character of your choice.

DOT COMMANDS AND PRINT FORMATTING

Dot Command Character. This is the character that begins a dot command and is also normally a period. Under some circumstances you might wish to use a different character.

Non-Break Space Character. Normally ^O, this character prints as a space, but is not treated as a word break by word wrap or paragraph reform. Any ASCII character may be used. For instance, the accent mark (hex 60) is a handy substitute if not used for its usual purpose, saving a keystroke.

Dots-On Flag. Disables dot command interpretation during editing if set to off, including effect of .LH command on page-break display; normally no reason to change.

HYPHENATION CRITERIA

Hyphenation Zone. This zone at the end of a line determines if a stop is to be made for proposed hyphenation of a word which is too long to fit, or if the word will be moved by word-wrap to the next line. The value entered sets the number of columns short of the right margin where the zone begins. It applies when hyphenation help is on. Make it larger for fewer stops and more ragged right margins, or smaller to be sure each line is more nearly filled out. Large values can result in excessive spacing of words and characters when justification is on, especially with narrow column widths.

Vowel Table Address. Starting address of special vowel table, entered with least-significant-byte first. Must be changed if you modify the starting address of this or following non-consonant table. If you add special vowel characters, for example, address of the following portion will be affected.

Non-Consonant Table Address. For regular vowels; see above comments.

Vowel And Non-Consonant Tables. This is essentially one table, although for addressing purposes it is treated like two. It is used to determine where the cursor is positioned when a hyphenation stop occurs—normally between two consonants or between a vowel and a following consonant. The first part contains special vowels, including those which are accented in some European languages. The second part contains standard English vowels. Three bytes at the end are available for expansion. You must maintain at least one zero byte at the end to terminate the table.

SPECIAL CHARACTERS DISPLAYED WHILE EDITING

Flag Characters. The following eight bytes are entries for characters which are displayed in the right-most screen column to indicate information about a line. All these may be changed, but normally you would have no need to do so except under special circumstances. Carriage return indicators may be an exception if you wish to create a version of WordStar for use in writing program source files. Soft carriage returns (blanks) are those entered by word-wrap. They do not display, and they move automatically as required whenever you use paragraph reform. Hard carriage returns display as a left-arrow (less-than) character and remain unless you move or delete them. For program files you may wish to use a blank for hard carriage returns and some other character for soft carriage returns (normally not used in such files).

Soft Hyphen Character. This character normally displays as a highlighted hyphen. That is, 80 hex is added to the hex value of the standard ASCII character. (See table A-2 for hex values of other highlighted characters.)

Block And Place Markers. The following 15 bytes are used for text marker characters, such as those for block identifiers and place markers; all are displayed in text between left and right arrows. Only the appropriate letters or numbers are entered here. They are numbered internally from 1 through 15, which has no external significance.

The first two are the beginning and ending block marks, <B> and <K>. A logical change might be to substitute E for K, although such a change would be usually irrelevant on the PC since the block end marker does not display unless you err and enter it in text before you have marked the beginning of a block. These markers will also display if only one is set or if both are set in the same place.

Two of the next three are used internally for cursor positioning when ^QP or ^QV commands are issued. Do not attempt to make these displayable. The third is not currently used.

The last ten are for in-text place markers using numerals 0 through 9. Normally there is little reason to modify these, although you conceivably might want to assign alphabetic characters as mnemonic reminders if your use of place markers follows some generally set pattern.

DEFAULTS FOR PRINTING OPTIONS

There are several entries you can use here for presets to questions asked by the program when you initiate printing of a file. A 00 entry means a default of no; an entry of FF means yes. With entries keyed to your normal printing procedure you can save time and keystrokes, since you will then be able to simply turn the printer on, press P, type the file name, and press Escape to start printing.

The first field is for disk file output; the normal default is no. If you make this a yes answer, the program will ask for a name of the output file. The next is for form feeds; if you customarily use fan-fold paper, you will want to make this a yes. Normally you will want to leave the suppress-page-formatting entry a no; otherwise, WordStar will not interpret and execute your embedded format commands. If you generally use cut sheets of paper, you will probably want to change the next default to a yes; it inserts a printer pause at the end of each page so that you can change paper. This completes basic entries for the print-initiation dialog.

The following entry allows you to suppress altogether the question, "Use form feeds?" in the print dialog by entering an FF. If you have set up defaults for your usual printing mode, this entry is largely irrelevant.

The omit-page-numbers entry can be set to FF to suppress the automatic inclusion of page numbers. If you want no page numbers at all, or prefer to have them elsewhere than bottom-centered, this is a useful change. You can still use page numbers as desired in a heading or footing by using a # character, or turn regular page numbering back on with a .PN command.

Merge-Printing Characters. These entries can be used to modify various special characters used in MailMerge. Included are the comma used as a data separator within a line, the double quote enclosing values containing commas and leading and trailing blanks, and the ampersand beginning and ending a variable. Also included are the character, normally a slash, separating a variable name from a following option letter, and the option letter to omit a line if the variable is a null.

CHANGING PROGRAM FILE NAMES

You can rename any of the WordStar program files if you wish, and there is at least one good reason to do so. If you want to use an electronic disk drive in memory, there is an advantage to having all the program files begin with the same prefix, such as WS. The copy command that loads your program files from floppy to RAM disk can then be just a single line in the batch file: **copy ws*.*** to whatever drive letter you select. This makes your autoexec batch file simpler, and it will execute a little faster.

If you rename any of the files, be sure to observe and follow the name format. The field begins with a zero byte, followed by the main part of the label, such as WS or WSOVLY1. The extension following the period is at the end of the field, and the period itself is omitted. Any space between is filled with zero bytes (00). If you wish to use an electronic disk drive and include MailMerge, a suggested substitute name is WSMAILMROVR, entered in this form. The SecMod program (Norton Utilities) will allow you to enter new names directly without converting to hex.

Remember that the name must be changed in two places: here and the external name of the file on your working program diskette. The external name should be in its usual format (for example, WSMAILMR.OVR), and names must be the same in both places except for the format differences. The reason is that names entered here are what WordStar looks for externally when loading or reloading files. External name changes are made in the usual way from the DOS prompt.

Table 6-1. Addresses Of Default Functions (WS.COM)

Addr	*Std Val*	*Function*	*Notes*
0360	03	Initial Help level	
0361	FF	Suppress Help level message	Patch 00 for on
0362	FF	Insert toggle (On)	Patch 00 for off
0363	FF	Opening Menu directory (On)	Patch 00 for off
0364	00 00	Reserved for expansion	
		*** Page Format ***	(2)
0366	08	Standard line height in 48ths	
0367	42	Standard page lgth in lines (66)	
0368	10 02	Page lgth in 48ths (8 X 66)	(3)
036A	08	Standard line height repeated	
036B	03	Top margin in lines	
036C	18 00	Top margin in 48ths (8 X 3)	(3)
036E	08	Standard line height repeated	
036F	02	Heading margin in lines	
0370	10 00	Heading margin in 48ths (8 X 2)	(3)
0372	08	Standard line height repeated	
0373	08	Bottom margin in lines	
0374	40 00	Bottom margin in 48ths (8 X 8)	(3)
0376	08	Standard line height repeated	
0377	02	Footing margin in lines	
0378	10 00	Footing margin in 48ths (8 X 2)	(3)
037A	08	Standard line height repeated	
037B	00	Zero for standard character width	
037C	0C	Std char width in 120ths: 1/10 in.	
037D	0A	Alt char width in 120ths: 1/12 in.	
037E	08	Printed page offset in characters	
		*** Margin Settings And S'script Roll ***	(2)
037F	00	Initial left margin col, minus 1	
0380	40	Initial right margin col, minus 1	
0381	03	Initial sub/superscript roll in 48ths	
0382	00 00 00	Reserved for expansion	
		*** Initial Editing Defaults ***	(2)
0385	FF	Word-wrap on/off (On)	Patch 00 for off
0386	FF	Justification on/off (On)	Patch 00 for off
0387	FF	Variable Tabs on/off (On)	Patch 00 for off

Table 6-1. Addresses Of Default Functions (Continued)

Addr	*Std Val*	*Function*	*Notes*
0388	00	Soft Hyphens on/off (Off)	Patch FF for on
0389	FF	Hyphen Help on/off (On)	Patch 00 for off
038A	FF	Display formatting chars (On)	Patch 00 for off
038B	FF	Display ruler line (On)	Patch 00 for off
038C	FF	Collect page-break data (On)	Patch 00 for off
038D	FF	Display page breaks (On)	Patch 00 for off
038E	01	Line spacing (sgl)	02 for dbl, etc.
038F	00	Block move mode (normal)	FF for col mode
0390	00 00	Reserved for expansion	
0392	00	Open file in document mode	FF for non-doc
0393	2E	Decimal tab aligning char	Decimal point
0394	00	Reserved for expansion	
		*** Dot Commands And Print Formatting ***	(2)
0395	2E	Dot command, initial char	Decimal point
0396	0F	Non-break space char	^O
0397	FF	Enable dot command displays	00 to disable
0398	00 00	Reserved for expansion	
		*** Hyphenation Criteria ***	(2)
039A	04	Hyphen-zone (cols at line end)	
039B	9F 03	Address of special vowel table	(3)
039D	A4 03	Address of regular vowel table	(3)
039F	59	Letter Y (vowel or consonant)	
03A0	5B 5D 7B 7D	Accented vowel chars:	[ ] { }
03A4	41 45 49 4F 55	Regular vowels:	A E I O U
03A9	00	Zero terminates table	
03AA	00 00 00	Reserved for table expansion	
		*** Special Characters Displayed While Editing ***	(2)
03AD	2E	End-of-file character	Period
03AE	3A	Beginning-of-file character	Colon
03AF	2B	Line longer than screen width	+
03B0	2D	Next line will overprint	–
03B1	4A	Line ends in LF without CR	J
03B2	50	Line is last line of page	P
03B3	20	Line ends in soft CR	blank
03B4	3C	Line ends in hard CR	<

Table 6-1. Addresses Of Default Functions (Continued)

Addr	*Std Val*	*Function*	*Notes*
03B5	4D	Line contains Merge dot com.	M
03B6	00 00	Reserved for expansion	
03B8	AD	Soft hyphen char (highlighted)	–
03B9	2D	Char for page-break line	–
03BA	42	Char for Begin-Block marker	B
03BB	4B	Char for End-Block marker	K
03BC	00	Internal mkr for cursor pos'g	Do not change
03BD	00	Internal mkr for find/rpl	Do not change
03BE	00	Internal marker #5	Unused
03BF	30 31 32 33	In-text place markers, 0-9	0 1 2 3
03C3	34 35 36 37	(Set/hide with ^K0-^K9)	4 5 6 7
03C7	38 39		8 9
03C9	00	Reserved for expansion	
		*** Defaults For Printing Options ***	(2)
03CA	00	Disk File Output? Y/N	Patch FF for Yes
03CB	00	Use Form Feeds? Y/N	Patch FF for Yes
03CC	00	Suppress Page Formatting? Y/N	Patch FF for Yes
03CD	00	Pause Between Pages? Y/N	Patch FF for Yes
03CE	00 00 00	Reserved for expansion	
03D1	00	Display "Use Form Feeds?"	FF to suppress
03D2	00	Reserved for expansion	
03D3	00	Omit standard page numbers	Patch FF to omit
03D4	FF	.UJ dot command enable	00 to disable
03D5	FF	Bidirectional printing enable	00 to disable
03D6	00 00	Reserved for expansion	
03D8	2C	Data value separator	, (merge-print)
03D9	22	Double quote delimiter	" (merge-print)
03DA	00	Reserved for expansion	
03DB	26	Char to begin variable	& (merge-print)
03DC	26	Char to end variable	& (merge-print)
03DD	2A	Char to omit line	* (obsolete)
03DE	2F	Separator for option letters	/ (merge-print)
03DF	4F	Char to omit line if vbl null	O (merge-print)
03E0	00 00 00	Reserved for expansion	
03E3	00 00 00	Reserved for expansion	

Table 6-1. Addresses Of Default Functions (Continued)

Addr	Std Val	Function	Notes	
		*** Program File Names ***	(2)	
03E6	00 57 53 20	Main program name	WS	COM
03EA	20 20 20 20	(observe format if renaming)		
03EE	20 43 4F 4D			
03F2	00 57 53 4D	Menu and message text file	WSMSGS	OVR
03F6	53 47 53 20	(observe format if renaming)		
03FA	20 4F 56 52			
03FE	00 57 53 4F	Overlay file	WSOVLY1	OVR
0402	56 4C 59 31	(observe format if renaming)		
0406	20 4F 56 52			
040A	00 4D 41 49	MailMerge overlay file	MAILMRGE	OVR
040E	4C 4D 52 47	(observe format if renaming)		
0412	45 4F 56 52			
0416	00 00 00 00	Reserved for expansion		
041A	00 00 00 00			
041E	00 00 00 00			

Notes:

(1) Addresses apply to WS.COM versions 3.3, 3.24, and most earlier versions for MS/PC-DOS.
(2) See corresponding heading in text for discussion.
(3) Values greater than one byte in length are entered with least-significant-byte first.

7

USING KEYBOARD ENHANCERS

If you have never used a keyboard enhancer before, your first question may be, "What are they?" In essence they are utility programs. They do not perform complete applications in the way, for example, that word processors do. Rather, they carry out auxiliary tasks in support of the main program. One of their uses is to modify the operator's keyboard interface with that program, and in so doing, they can provide substantial benefits.

First, they are great timesavers because of the number of keystrokes they can eliminate. The better ones go further than merely allowing you to condense multiple-keystroke commands into simpler ones; they permit use of what are known as keyboard macros. Originating from Greek, the term macro means large or extended. Hence, a keyboard macro is a long phrase or string of characters that, once entered, can be recalled and inserted at will with only a couple of keystrokes. Macros are especially useful for saving and recalling complex commands or repetitive strings of text or data.

Second, and perhaps even more useful, keyboard enhancers can be used to restructure a program's command set and to reassign commands to different keys. Instead of ^PB for boldface, for instance, you could make the command simply Alt-B; it's faster and saves a keystroke. Similarly, you can assign three new sets of shifted function key commands using the Alt, Caps shift, and Ctrl keys. Any of these can be multiple commands; it all depends on how you make the assignments.

Before you get the idea that keyboard enhancers rank with the greatest inventions in computing history, however, let's consider their limitations. They work by intercepting keystrokes from the keyboard and transforming them into other characters before sending them to the main application program. In this sense they are translators. They reinterpret existing commands, assign them to other keys, and create text or command strings, or produce combinations of these functions.

While these are no small accomplishments, enhancers cannot create new commands in a logic sense, nor can they reset default operating values or other internal program parameters. Functionally speaking, you are bound by whatever capabilities the main program makes available through the keyboard. Moreover, an enhancer does require memory space and must be loaded at start-up time just as any other program. Given growing memory capacities and the long term downward cost trend of memory devices, the extra space required may be a small consideration for your home or office installation. But it could be a factor if you also want to use an electronic disk drive, or if you use a portable machine having limited memory.

The bottom line, then, is that a keyboard enhancer is not a panacea but is a useful adjunct to many kinds of main programs. Certainly this is true with WordStar. A good enhancer can help you do things that otherwise would be inconvenient if not highly impractical. The clincher is cost; compared to the prices of major programs, keyboard enhancers are cheap.

PROKEY AND WORDSTAR - A HAPPY COMBINATION

Although there are other keyboard enhancers on the market, ProKey is the most popular by a wide margin—perhaps due largely to its popularity with WordStar users. Whether this bespeaks a superior product or astute marketing, or both, is difficult to determine. It suffices, however, to note that ProKey does the job and is an excellent companion to WordStar. Enhancers in general work in similar ways, and if you prefer another, the following material should still prove useful.

Rather than rehash the basics of using ProKey, which you can get from the manual, we will concentrate on how it can be used to advantage with WordStar. We'll also look at how you can use WordStar itself to set up your ProKey files. As mentioned in chapters 3 and 4, adding shifted function keys or modifying basic WordStar commands so that the Alt key can be used is very difficult to do directly. You can easily change the unshifted function keys, or modify commands prefixed by control-shifted characters, but the easiest way to go beyond that point is with a keyboard enhancer.

Why not simply do it all with ProKey? You can, but there is a price. For each ProKey command you add, you must also add another line to your key definition file, so the file gets larger and uses more memory. As the file grows, more time is consumed in scanning it each time you issue a command. Although the loss in execution speed may not be glaring, it is real. Probably the best overall trade-off, therefore, is to make directly in WordStar whatever changes you can and to use ProKey for the rest.

Shifted Function Keys. Added to the ten basic function key assignments provided for by WordStar, you can create with ProKey a full set of ten more function keys in combination with each of the three shift keys on the PC keyboard: Alt, Caps, and Ctrl. Thus you can have a total of up to forty function keys. Each key can execute one command or multiple commands, depending on how you define it. Access to them, of course, is then with F1 through F10 alone, Alt-F1 through Alt-F10, Caps-F1 through Caps-F10, and Ctrl-F1 through Ctrl-F10.

This is a lot of commands, possibly more than you would want or should assign to function keys. Although your first impulse in the delight of being able to do it may be to "fill 'em up," these assignments call for a certain amount of reflection and planning. There is little to be gained in creating such a welter of function keys that they are hard to remember or that they keep your fingers constantly moving away from the main part of the keyboard. We will take up these considerations in the next chapter.

Modifying Commands. Criticisms of WordStar often center on the number of keystrokes required for frequently used commands, or on the particular combination of keys required. It takes a minimum of four key depressions, for example, to reset left or right margins or to set or clear a tab stop. Further, some typists find certain key combinations, such as ^Q, awkward or difficult to reach. Fixing these shortcomings is a natural for ProKey.

With ProKey you can redefine margin commands, such as ^OL-Escape, to simply Alt-L, and its right-margin companion to Alt-R. Similarly, you could change the Find String command from ^QF to simply Alt-F. Another potential application is to simplify pitch changes and other print-formatting commands such as bold, underscore, and so on. The intent of these examples, however, is only to convey a general idea of possibilities rather than to suggest specific changes. Again, to avoid the risk of a hodge-podge, planning before action should be the order of activity.

Since ProKey does not actually change a command, but only adds another version of it, the original WordStar command is still usable. Therefore, none of the menu prefixes (^K, ^O, ^P, and ^Q) are disabled, so you can still roll down a help menu by entering the appropriate prefix. This is helpful when you need to refer to infrequently used commands for which you have not assigned ProKey alternates. You will need to maintain a help level not lower than 2 for this, but for ProKey-issued commands, the menus will never display because the second of two-character commands is dispatched before the message time-out occurs. (This is explained in more detail in Chapter 11.)

CREATING PROKEY DEFINITION FILES

To use ProKey with WordStar you must have two related files on your working WordStar diskette—the ProKey program itself and a file of key definitions. The latter you must create. You can do this using ProKey in its on-line or "recorder" mode, or by using an "off-line" technique in which you first create, proof, and edit the definition file before using it. The off-line approach has at least two advantages. You can use WordStar to create this file, giving you a full range of familiar editing capabilities, and you can use temporary ProKey macros to eliminate repetitive keystrokes as you build this file. (If you are not familiar with the basics of these techniques, refer to the ProKey manual.)

Assuming you are going to use the off-line approach, let's begin by looking at the mechanics of creating a key assignment, in particular how a definition appears in your ProKey definition file. As an example, we'll assume you wish to assign to Alt-F1 the WordStar commands to save your currently open file to disk and return to the end of that file so you can continue writing. The required commands are ^KS and ^QC. The format of the definition is as follows:

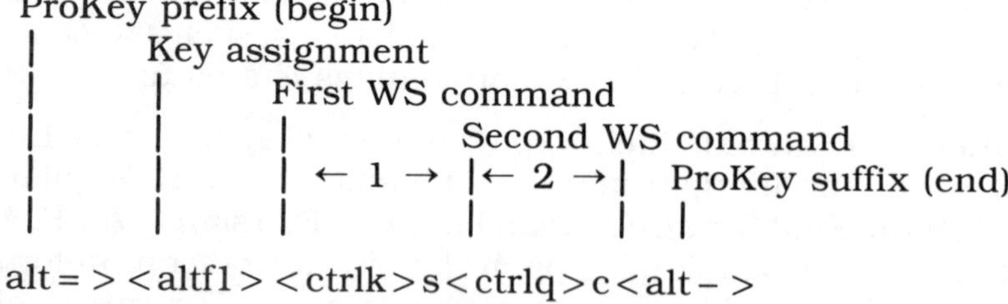

<alt=> <altf1> <ctrlk>s<ctrlq>c<alt->

The bottom line of this example illustrates the actual content as it would appear in your file. Note that several items are enclosed by left and right arrow symbols ("less-than" and "greater-than" symbols, if you prefer) and that certain keys are represented by abbreviations. These are ProKey conventions for defining key names and/or combinations, and they allow a definition file to be built off-line without executing the actual commands. They visually isolate individual elements for convenience in proofing as well. You should also note that in the off-line mode you type these entries exactly as shown. ProKey's admonitions not to type the key names or include the arrow symbols apply only in the on-line mode.

As shown in the preceding example, the first element in a definition is the prefix <alt = >. This prefix must be included at the beginning of each line. Next is the key or combination which initiates the modified command or text string; it must be one that ProKey recognizes for this purpose and is always enclosed in left and right arrows. Following are the WordStar commands (this could also be a text or data string) you wish to assign to that key. These can range from a single command to any number you want to be executed. Again, note that ProKey requires shifted keys to be enclosed by arrow symbols. In the case of two-character commands, the second is not enclosed since it is interpreted literally. The final element is the suffix <alt – >, which signifies to ProKey the end of a definition.

USING WORDSTAR TO CREATE A DEFINITION FILE

By using the non-document mode, you can create key definition files quickly and easily with WordStar. You can assign any file name you wish, but something mnemonic like Keydef will help you remember what the file is later when you see it in the directory. A filename extension is to a degree excess baggage at this point, but you can use one if you wish.

A sample definition file is shown in table 7-1. Be sure you follow the format illustrated in the left-hand column of this example when actually creating a definition file. The right-hand column and the column headings are included only to make the example easier to understand. Do not include material like this in an actual file.

Each ProKey definition is placed on a single line terminated by a hard carriage return. If a definition is longer than a single screen-width, simply let it extend to the right, and complete it before you insert the carriage return. Under most circumstances you can have an embedded carriage return in the middle of a definition, but it is less complicated to do the other way. Note also that each complete definition is separated from the following one by an asterisk in column 1 of the next line followed by a hard carriage return. You can include comments, such as a file creation or revision date, at the end of the file.

You can save considerable effort by using ProKey itself to assist in creating a definition file. If you have not already done so, you must first copy ProKey to your working WordStar diskette. Then from the DOS prompt enter **prokey/i** before initiating WordStar. If you are using a batch file for start-up, change it to include this entry, again before the command to initiate WordStar. (This change is temporary; later you will include the name of your newly-created definition file.) ProKey will then be installed and available whenever you need it.

Here is one way you can use ProKey to automatically type repetitive portions of your definition file. After you have entered the WordStar command characters in your first definition, do not type <alt – > as shown in the examples. Instead, you can set things up so that ProKey does some of the work. You will now use the "live" or on-line ProKey convention where items enclosed by left and right arrows are not typed literally but merely represent characters to be typed. Thus, <alt = > is actually typed by holding down the Alt key and pressing the = key. Then enter literally the items shown below in bold; they are keystrokes you will want ProKey to reproduce for you automatically as you build your key definition file. With this bit of explanation out of the way, type the following:

<alt = > <alt0> **<alt – >** <Ret> ***** <Ret> **<alt=> <** <alt – >

Note that when you type Alt= the cursor changes to a solid box shape, indicating that you are now in ProKey and it is waiting for you to enter an assignment key. In this example we used Alt0, but you could use any other valid combination. Verbally we would describe the remaining entries as follows: type **<alt – >**, press enter (ProKey nomenclature for the return key), type an asterisk, press enter, type **<alt = > <**, press Alt – . As you type the characters shown in bold they appear on-screen, and the <return> entries will start new lines.

With the final entry you are now back in regular WordStar. Note that the cursor reverts to its usual form. You will also note that in the process of entering the preceding ProKey string you have completed the key definition you previously started and have begun the next definition. (You have also created a keyboard macro.) Type the assignment key for the next command and the appropriate WordStar command characters, as you did in the first line. When you finish, press Alt-0. The display shown below should appear automatically, <alt – > appearing at the end of your last WordStar command entry in the definition line. If it doesn't come out this way, do not be discouraged; simply restart as above, and redefine your macro.

(your key definition)<alt – >
*

<alt = > <

Actually this is a fairly simple macro, but it demonstrates the process and is effective as well. By organizing your definitions into groups based on similarity of required inputs (i.e., the alt-shifted function keys in one group, the control-shifted keys in another, etc.) you can make ProKey do even more work. The ultimate time and keystroke saver is to use variable fields as explained in the ProKey manual, although the preceding example is easier if you have not used variable fields before.

Complete your key definition file, and save it to disk. With a few final steps you will then be ready to start using your ProKey-customized version of WordStar. First, copy your definition file to your working copy of WordStar. If you are using an autoexec or other batch file for start-up (recommended procedure), modify that file to invoke ProKey and your key definition file. Include the following command line before the line that invokes WordStar: **prokey filename/r**. The filename is the name of your key definition file. Now use and enjoy.

USING PROKEY WITH DOS

Although this might be considered a digression from our main theme, it really isn't. WordStar customizing involves frequent exits to DOS for formatting new diskettes, copying files, creating or modifying batch files, rearranging file order for improved efficiency, and so forth. Many of the same operations accompany normal WordStar usage as well, and anything we can do to speed them up and reduce effort is to our advantage. Moreover, the techniques described generally apply to WordStar also.

ProKey is just as good at saving keystrokes in DOS as it is with WordStar. How many times, for example, have you typed FORMAT B: or CHKDSK or COPY A:*.* B:? With ProKey you can assign all these commands and more to function keys, saving dozens of keystrokes and avoiding typing errors in the bargain. This can justify ProKey's cost by itself.

Table 7-2 illustrates what you can do with comparatively little thought or effort. This table is actually a file, created with WordStar, that is displayed each time DOS is booted or whenever function key F1 is pressed at the DOS prompt. F2 issues a ^C, which cancels the DOS command initiated by any other function key. Where DOS commands do not contain a built-in pause, commands assigned to other function keys are deliberately left incomplete by one keystroke so that they can be cancelled if a wrong key is pressed—not exactly a remote possibility during late-night sessions.

Although this example uses only unshifted and Alt-shifted function keys, you can assign Caps-shifted and Ctrl-shifted function keys too, or any other

ProKey-recognized combinations. Of course you are not limited to just DOS commands; you can use this scheme also to invoke other programs such as utilities. Another application is simply to play back long phrases like **copy con: autoexec.bat** or to include remarks.

As with WordStar, using ProKey with DOS in this way requires you to create a key definition file. Again, using WordStar and appropriate ProKey macros speeds up and simplifies this task considerably. To illustrate the complete process begun with table 7-2, and the correlation between the two parts, the related key definition file is presented in table 7-3.

The first entry in this file assigns to function key F1 a DOS command to type to the screen the file DOSPRO.DOC, which is the name of the file shown in table 7-2. The second entry assigns to F2 a ^C command, which interrupts a pending DOS command and returns you to the DOS prompt. The assignment to F6 is similar to the one already assigned to that key by DOS: a ^Z, or end-of-file mark. The difference is that an <enter> is included after the ^Z, saving a keystroke. An <enter> is also included for commands that already pause before full execution, such as FORMAT and DISKCOPY. For those that do not, such as COPY *.*, the <enter> is omitted, providing an opportunity to cancel if one of these commands is initiated by mistake. In other words, exact content of a definition is dictated by what would happen if the command were accidentally executed. The objective is to make any mistakes failsafe, for there is obviously little gain in risking the loss of valuable work to save a keystroke or two.

The last steps are to copy your screen display and definition files to your DOS diskette and to create an appropriate batch file for start-up. The following would be suitable for the examples shown:

```
copy con: autoexec.bat
date
time
prokey doskey.def/r
type dospro.doc
^Z
```

If you have an expansion board with clock module, you will want to substitute the appropriate clock command for date and time. And of course you can add commands for any other functions you customarily invoke as part of your DOS start-up routine.

As a final thought to conclude this chapter, it is worth noting that examples presented here have only scratched the surface. They are not necessarily intended to be used literally but to illustrate techniques and to stimulate your own ideas. In the hands of an ingenious user, a good enhancer program is a capable tool—not only for use with WordStar but in other ways as well.

Table 7-1. Example ProKey Definitions For WordStar

Definition File Entry	*Interpretation*
<alt=><altf1><ctrlk>d<alt–>	Alt-F1 = ^KD
*	
<alt=><altf2><ctrlk>q<alt–>	Alt-F2 = ^KQ
*	
<alt=><altf3><ctrlq>p<alt–>	Alt-F3 = ^QP
*	
<alt=><altf4><ctrlk>w<alt–>	Alt-F4 = ^KW
*	
<alt=><altf5><ctrly><alt–>	Alt-F5 = ^Y
*	
<alt=><altf6><ctrlk>y<alt–>	Alt-F6 = ^KY
*	
<alt=><altf7><ctrlk>b<alt–>	Alt-F7 = ^KB
*	
<alt=><altf8><ctrlk>k<alt–>	Alt-F8 = ^KK
*	
<alt=><altf9><ctrlk>h<alt–>	Alt-F9 = ^KH
*	
<alt=><altf10><ctrlk>v<alt–>	Alt-F10 = ^KV
*	
<alt=><∧rgt><ctrlf><alt–>	Ctrl → = ^F
*	
<alt=><∧lft><ctrla><alt–>	Ctrl ← = ^A
*	
<alt=><alta><ctrlp>a<alt–>	Alt-A = ^PA
*	
<alt=><altl><ctrlo>l<esc><alt–>	Alt-L = ^OL(Esc)

Table 7-2. Example Screen Display (DOSPRO.DOC)

```
                  DOS FUNCTION KEY ASSIGNMENTS

DISPLAY KEYS -------- F1      F2 --------  CANCEL COMMAND
bulkerase b:/b        Alt     Alt          copy2pc a: b:

DIRECTORY A: -------- F3      F4 --------  DIRECTORY B:
dir/w a:              Alt     Alt          dir/w b:

FORMAT B: ----------- F5      F6 --------  ^Z (EOF mark)
format b:/s           Alt     Alt          copy con: auto.bat

DISKCOPY A: B: ------ F7      F8 --------  DISKCOPY B: A:
copy a:*.* b:         Alt     Alt          copy b:*.* a:

CHKDSK A: ----------- F9      F10 -------  CHKDSK B:
diskcomp a: b:        Alt     Alt          diskcomp b: a:
```

Table 7-3. Example Key Definition File (DOSKEY.DEF)

```
<alt=><f1>type dospro.doc<enter><alt->
*
<alt=><f2><ctrlc><alt->
*
<alt=><f3>DIR A:<enter><alt->
*
<alt=><f4>DIR B:<enter><alt->
*
<alt=><f5>FORMAT B:<enter><alt->
*
<alt=><f6><ctrlz><enter><alt->
*
<alt=><f7>DISKCOPY A: B:<enter><alt->
*
<alt=><f8>DISKCOPY B: A:<enter><alt->
*
<alt=><f9>CHKDSK A:<enter><alt->
*
<alt=><f10>CHKDSK B:<enter><alt->
*
```

Table 7-3. Example Key Definition File (Continued)

```
<alt=><altf1>BULKERAS B:/B<enter> <alt->
*
<alt=><altf2>COPY2PC A: B:<enter> <alt->
*
<alt=><altf3>DIR/W A:<enter> <alt->
*
<alt=><altf4>DIR/W B:<enter> <alt->
*
<alt=><altf5>FORMAT B:/S<enter> <alt->
*
<alt=><altf6>copy con: autoexec.bat<enter> <alt->
*
<alt=><altf7>COPY A:*.* B:     press Return to begin<alt->
*
<alt=><altf8>COPY B:*.* A:     press Return to begin<alt->
*
<alt=><altf9>DISKCOMP A: B:<enter> <alt->
*
<alt=><altf10>DISKCOMP B: A:<enter> <alt->
*
File updated 9-9-84
```

8
PUTTING IT ALL TOGETHER

If you have read or at least skimmed the preceding chapters, you are now aware that the scope of possible changes and personal enhancements to WordStar is broad indeed. Many modifications described may have elicited an "Aha!" followed by prompt action to put them to good use. Although you might be satisfied to quit there, chances are as good that all this has been merely a prelude to a larger customizing project. If so, a question you will soon face is how to get it all together.

Our primary focus in this chapter is on integrating enhancements which, as an aid to clarity, we have previously considered separately. We will also cover some other helpful techniques for the first time. These include creating separate customized versions of the program for different jobs, using electronic disk drives to speed up program operation, and how to use batch files to simplify start-up routines.

The following chapters contain more information on useful changes, but most of this material treats topics you can deal with more or less on their own. This is not so with function keys, command structures, messages and menus, editing defaults, and keyboard enhancers. Each influences the others in some way or is affected by them. We have discussed at several points the implications of key assignments and modified commands. As we have seen, keyboard enhancers open up another dimension of possibilities, and with them a new series of choices. Putting all this together in a cohesive way requires treating the elements and the process as an entity.

When you have specific changes in mind, like altering the backspace key to delete characters, the requirement and the technique are clear and unambiguous. But how to deal with a group of related keys or operations, or even to recognize that perhaps they should be handled as a family, can be a good deal less obvious. After all, professional program designers sometimes miss the mark themselves. So spending time to ponder all the implications will generally pay off.

PRACTICAL INTEGRATION CONSIDERATIONS

If you have already fixed your pet peeves and want to go on to more ambitious changes but don't have a firm approach in mind, it is recommended that you read the latter part of Chapter 2. Making notes as suggested there can help clarify your initial ideas. A review of relevant parts of Chapters 3, 4, and 7 may also prove helpful. If a clear picture of your own usage patterns does not emerge, feel free to experiment and try some arrangement a while. Using it will tell you whether or not it's right. Very little is chiseled in stone, and any change you make can be undone. These trial runs can help you zero in on a setup that is best for you.

Function key assignments are where users often part company, except to agree that many of WordStar's stock assignments leave much to be desired. Here are some points to consider, some of which have been made before but are worth revisiting. Since multiple commands can be assigned to function keys, you can save keystrokes by doing so. On the other hand, reaching for function keys requires hand movement, which takes more time than pressing keys under your fingertips. Sometimes this is an advantage, as in delete operations. The mental pause involved can be just enough to stop you from making deletes you really didn't intend. You may feel that putting simple commands like ^T or ^Y on these keys wastes available capacity, but balance this against the time and effort it takes to retype a word or line deleted accidentally. You also have the rest of the keyboard to work with, and some commands might work better there.

Functional grouping of commands is desirable. If you make numerous block moves, for instance, consider the sequence of commands: mark the block beginning, move cursor, mark the end, move cursor, move block, hide block marks. If you can arrange the key assignments to minimize required physical movements, and if these motions seem natural and logical, you will save time and make fewer mistakes. On the subject of mistakes, it can be helpful in early stages of developing a layout to stop whenever you make errors while using the program and ask yourself why they occurred. A little analysis may point to a better approach.

If you opt for shifted function keys by using a keyboard enhancer, you can make assignments not only in groups of related commands but in families of groups. For instance, you might use unshifted function keys for commands you use frequently but for one reason or another you don't want to use as they appear on the main part of the keyboard. You can then use the various shifted combinations for other command groups you use less frequently but want to keep together. We've mentioned block commands; other possibilities include search and replace commands, margin and tab commands, and printed output formatting commands. Incidentally, there is no innate reason for assigning a full set of ten keys for a given shift combination; if it makes sense, fine—but don't do it just to fill up space.

The principal considerations for commands you leave on the main part of the keyboard are to save keystrokes and to choose keys which are easy to reach, based on the assumption that among these are commands you use most often. If you plan to use the Alt key and single letters, for example, it is good to choose letters that help you remember the function, such as L for left margin, R for right, etc. An exception might be in order for commands that insert a character on the screen, such as those for subscripts and superscripts, underline, and so on. Unless having different characters pop onto the screen does not bother you, there is an advantage in using the same final characters as the original commands, such as Alt-T for superscripts and Alt-S for underline, even though their mnemonic value is virtually nil. It visually links initiating action with result, providing reinforcement and helping to minimize errors.

For commands using a shift key and single letter there aren't enough characters to cover all possibilities, unless you use a large number of function keys. In addition, a specific character might logically apply to more than one command. Therefore you will have to make choices—the same problem faced by the original designers. One way of handling the problem is to assign alternates only for commands you use frequently. This results in having to use an amalgam of your abbreviated commands and regular WordStar commands, but it causes little difficulty in practice. It may even be a good trade-off, since you will then save many keystrokes on the frequently used commands but will use the others often enough to keep from forgetting standard commands entirely. For the latter it is sufficient to recall only the correct group if you leave the help level set at 2, since entering the prefix will cause its corresponding menu to scroll down.

Throughout this discussion and in preceding chapters phrases such as "moving commands" and "assigning commands" have been used freely. Lest there be any misconception, we are not actually changing the basic WordStar commands. When dealing with function keys we are merely assigning duplicate or multiple commands to these keys. The original commands as they appear on the main part of the keyboard are still active. When we use a keyboard enhancer to modify commands, we are creating alternate and hopefully simpler or easier commands. But again the original commands are also active; indeed they must be or the alternates would not work. The only exceptions to all this are changes we make directly to basic WordStar commands as described in Chapter 4. The practical effect, however, is largely the same as if we had actually made changes, since our minds and fingers learn the new patterns and the old fade from lack of use.

Because the original commands remain active, some degree of restraint in creating alternate commands is advisable. Among the best of WordStar's many good features is that the program almost never does anything unexpected or drastic when an invalid command is issued. Creating numerous alternate commands tends, in effect, to undermine this quality and increases chances for errors made through unintended keystrokes.

AN EXAMPLE ILLUSTRATING THE APPROACH

Figures 8-1 and 8-2 illustrate key assignments for a practical integrated approach using shifted function keys and the Alt key in combination with single letters for frequently used commands. Although this system works well and applies many of the considerations covered earlier, it is by no means held up as the optimum for all users. You may find a considerably different approach better suited to your personal style and needs. Its main purpose is to illustrate how the principles we have discussed can be applied to a real-world situation.

In this example most of the regular function keys have been redefined, and ProKey is used to provide a set of Alt-shifted function keys. It is also used to create a set of Alt-shifted alternates for often used commands on the main keyboard. As described in Chapter 7, a key definition file is required and is illustrated in figure 8-3. By referring to this listing you can easily see the relationships between new commands and their standard WordStar equivalents.

Let's begin by examining the function key assignments shown in figure 8-1. Most unshifted keys are changed from the usual WordStar setup to reduce keystrokes, to divorce the most often used delete commands from the main part of the keyboard, and to group several cursor control commands. Some of these commands are relatively simple in their basic WordStar form, but savings of just a stroke or two mount up. As previously discussed, saving keystrokes is not the only factor to consider. Assigned to F1 is the normal save-and-resume command (^KS), which is expanded to include a ^QC command to return the cursor to the end of the current file. Because F2 is located handily adjacent to the Escape key, a Cancel command is assigned to it, consisting of the normal ^U command and saving a keystroke. The command ^KR for reading external files is assigned to F4 and is renamed to indicate more precisely what it does. Its companion Alt-shifted version is ^KW. Cursor commands ^QS and ^QD are put on F7 and F8, overcoming the irritant of overshooting the ends of lines when using the arrow keys and eliminating the need to use the awkward keystrokes of the originals. Although there are compromises, the rationale behind these assignments was as much as possible to confine use of the central keyboard to text input operations.

A full set of Alt-shifted function keys are included. In general they are designed to complement the unshifted keys so that hand movement patterns for related functions are similar and become reinforced through repetition. A second objective was to centralize frequently used block commands. As an example of how this arrangement evolved, consider the steps usually required to move a paragraph: position the cursor to the paragraph beginning (F7), mark block beginning (Alt-F7), put the cursor at the paragraph end (F8), mark the end (Alt-F8), move block (Alt-F10), and hide block marks (Alt-F9). Although we have omitted cursor positioning steps using the right hand, you can see that the pattern for the left hand is simple and natural. If you can devise similar types of patterns for command groups they will be easier to learn and use, and they will economize on hand movements.

For frequently used commands on the main keyboard, a set of Alt-shifted keys is assigned as shown in figure 8-2. Each consists of a single shifted key, saving many keystrokes and in several cases improving the mnemonic relationship between key and command. For reasons discussed earlier, the choice of characters is influenced by on-screen appearance, if there is one. Using Alt-P as the print pause command instead of Alt-C is an exception, the latter having already been designated as the line centering command.

In a few instances all logical character choices had been used for other commands considered to be higher in priority. There is then little choice except to make arbitrary selections. You will probably find similar compromises necessary, but if the number can be kept small, you should have no problem.

CREATING MULTIPLE PROGRAM VERSIONS

Creating different custom versions of WordStar is easy to do, and it simplifies the logistics of dealing with multiple uses and more than one equipment configuration. Here is also a good place to give MicroPro credit for an enlightened and restrained approach to the thorny issue of copy protection. Without the ability to make additional working copies easily, customizing the program would be a more complicated task.

One of the handiest applications is to simplify the handling of printer interfaces. If you use more than one printer and they are different types, you can create multiple versions of WordStar which are identical except for the printer each will drive. Another possibility is to create versions for various print wheels of a daisy-wheel printer. Using the methods described in Chapter 11, you can fine tune the character spacing table in each version and obtain optimum results from any number of print wheels, both standard and proportional spacing.

If you do any programming, WordStar is an excellent tool for creating and editing source files. Simply using the non-document mode takes care of most of the mechanics, but you might still want to do some fine tuning for maximum ease of use. In particular you might duplicate some of the editing command modifications you have made to your writing version. Consistency between the two versions will tend to minimize mistakes and reduce the need for conscious thought about which one you are using.

An obvious application is to create separate versions for different kinds of writing tasks. From the standpoint of techniques at least, writing technical material and fiction are quite different (despite allegations of cynics that the results are often indistinguishable). Differences in the tools may be called for, but beware of carrying this too far; it would serve little useful purpose to develop such radically different versions of the program that becoming proficient with any is difficult.

Prominent and diligent labeling of different versions is an important practical consideration. Although this may seem too obvious to mention, it is easy to neglect, and reaching for the wrong version when you are going to edit an important text file invites disaster.

USING ELECTRONIC DISK DRIVES

As mentioned briefly before, using an electronic or RAM disk drive with WordStar is especially advantageous because of the program's many overlays. Repeatedly bringing these overlays in from a floppy disk slows down program operation substantially. You can also set up an electronic drive for use with your text files, but this involves risks of data loss that may outweigh the gain in speed.

In essence, setting up an electronic disk drive involves setting aside appropriate space in memory (hence the equivalent term RAM disk) and using a special utility program to implement it. DOS 2.0 and later versions include such a program, but you may prefer a more fully featured proprietary version of the type available from AST Research, Quadram, STB, and others. If you buy an expansion board made by one of these manufacturers, the necessary software is usually included with both memory boards and I/O boards.

It is not always necessary to add a memory board if you have a fully populated 256K system. If your RAM disk program allows for short drives, so called because they permit use of drives "short" of the normal single-sided or double-sided capacities, you can set up a 128K single-sided RAM disk and still have 128K of working space. (Not all programs provide this feature.) This is adequate space for most WordStar configurations, especially if you use DOS 1.1 which is smaller than later versions and works every bit as well for most word processing applications.

If you wish to set up electronic disks for both program and text files, it will be necessary to add a memory expansion board to gain the necessary space. Your text files will then be at risk due to power outages, even if they are only momentary. Program files can be reloaded, but any text you have not previously saved to floppy disk will be lost permanently. One way of averting this possibility is to buy an un-interruptible power supply, commonly known by its initials UPS. In the past UPS systems were bulky and expensive, but smaller and more economical units have begun to appear on the market. Most use small, sealed rechargeable batteries to cut cost and size. They provide only a few minutes' worth of backup power, but that is enough for you to transfer files to floppy disk. Whether the modest gain in speed a RAM disk provides for text files justifies the added expense and system complexity is for you to decide.

USING BATCH FILES FOR SIMPLIFIED START-UP

By the time you reach this point and if you have implemented many of the varied kinds of modifications and enhancements discussed, starting up can get to be a real chore. Operations like reading a real-time clock, if you use one, loading a RAM disk program and copying all your WordStar files to an electronic drive, and loading ProKey and related definition files add up to a lot of keystrokes if you tried to do it manually. The obvious answer is to use an autoexec batch file for start-up.

If you are well versed in using batch files you can skip this part, but if not, it may be helpful. The following is an example autoexec batch file which illustrates the techniques. You may not use this exact configuration of programs but from it you should get the general idea. It is shown as if you were going to create it from scratch, so it includes the DOS prompts and opening and ending commands.

```
A> copy con: autoexec.bat
   clock
   superdrv c:/1
   copy ws*.* c:              (see note in text about this line)
   prokey keydef/r
   b:
   c:ws
   ^Z
A>
```

There is somewhat more to this file than meets the eye. We've used a few simple tricks to simplify it and make it and the whole system execute a trifle faster. Following the opening autoexec.bat instruction are commands to read date and time from the clock and set up the electronic disk drive. These are based on AST hardware and software, so if you're using another brand the commands will be different. The astclock command was abbreviated to simply clock, with a corresponding change to the program name. The next command sets up a single-sided RAM disk as drive C. Then we copy the WordStar programs from floppy drive A to electronic drive C, followed by a command to initiate ProKey and read the key definition file into memory. Then we designate drive B as the logged drive, for that is where our text files will be located. Finally, we cause WS.COM to load from drive C and end the file with a ^Z (F6 on the PC keyboard).

For all this to work properly a few changes are necessary. First we must respecify the default drive entry in WS.COM from A to C as described in Chapter 11. (In 3.3 it can also be done from WINSTALL.) By designating the electronic disk as drive C and making it the WordStar program default drive, we need transfer only the main programs WS.COM, WSMSGS, and WSOVLY1 to take advantage of its speed in WordStar operations. This minimizes the memory space required for drive C. If you include MailMerge, you can rename it as described in Chapter 6 to retain the simplicity and speed of using the ws*.* command line. (To use this command, you will either have to rename other WS-prefixed files you do not want to transfer, such as WSCOLOR.BAS, etc., or omit them from your boot diskette. The latter is preferred.) Remaining programs are left to load from drive A, since frequent access will normally not be required. You can keep several other utility programs on drive A (such as Chkdsk), and they will be readily accessible from WordStar with the R command at the Opening Menu. In this case remember to include the A: drive prefix when you respond to the prompt for the program name.

As a final refinement you might want to check the order of programs on your working diskette. If you arrange these in their order of loading, they will load slightly faster with a little less wear and tear on your disk drive. Using the DOS Copy command to do this provides a small bonus—if any files have become fragmented it will rearrange them in contiguous sectors.

DOCUMENTING YOUR CHANGES

Considering how often we are objects of exhortations to pay attention to documentation needs, there must be some rebellious streak in human nature that entices us all to ignore them. Yet there are at least two good reasons for heeding such advice—both in our own self-interest: documentation makes a modified program much easier to use, and it can save us from a lot of misery if disaster strikes and we are forced to reconstruct an elaborate set of program modifications we may have spent hours or days creating.

Figures 8-1 and 8-2 illustrate the front and back sides of a handy kind of command reference card you can easily create. Once you have settled on a modified command structure, it is easy to capture the details and produce such a reference card using WordStar itself. For very little cost or effort you can even take a printout to a local quick-copy shop, have it copied to front and back on colored card stock, and have it sealed in plastic. It will look professional and will serve you and any other users well.

Making a record of your program patches is even easier. At a minimum, you should make periodic printed dumps as you progress with changes; methods are described in Chapter 2. With little extra effort you can produce, using WordStar, a handier documentation file as illustrated in figure 8-4.

The exact form of your records is relatively unimportant; recording the data is what matters. Even a simple log can help you avoid the futility of trying to recall details of changes you may have made months earlier.

PROGRAMS TO ROUND OUT YOUR SYSTEM

More recently arrived on the market is a class of programs which have been dubbed "desk-top" utilities. Their purpose is to provide automated assistance in handling a wide range of nitty-gritty details that attend or otherwise interrupt the main flow of work. Telephones ring and generate other telephone calls or notes to be saved, the text you're working on needs a number that must be calculated, you need to know on what day of the week a particular date fell four years ago, or you want to make an ASCII-to-hex conversion and have misplaced your printed table, and on it goes.

These programs sit unobtrusively in the background waiting for your summons to deal with the above and other distractions. By opening a window in your main program and closing it when you finish, they are quick and efficient, minimizing disruptions in your primary train of thought. This can be a valuable addition to your word processing system.

Among the most popular of these programs is Borlund's Sidekick, which has a feature especially useful to WordStar customizers. Not only does it use the basic WordStar command set, its installation routine permits you to install modified commands including those using shifted keys. Thus you can use the same custom editing commands you have devised for WordStar. The way you do this is to load Sidekick's installation routine and at the proper menu select the editing command table. At each command prompt, enter the key combination you have selected for your corresponding WordStar command. For example, if you wish to use Alt-F7 to set the block-begin marker, press those keys at the appropriate prompt. Due to the way Sidekick interprets keystrokes, the displayed response is not Alt-F7, but that combination is activated. A keyboard enhancer is not required to accomplish this, and the feature extends to other Borlund products such as Turbo Pascal.

We've already covered use of keyboard enhancers to implement otherwise impractical command changes in WordStar but have only touched their other capabilities. Coupled with a desk-top utility, such a combination provides and in some ways exceeds conveniences found in integrated software systems like Symphony and Framework, without compromising your freedom of choice. Be aware, though, that bringing all this together can create compatibility problems. These can be most acute in your choice of desk-top utilities and keyboard enhancers. For this as well as obvious marketing reasons, Borlund recommends using Sidekick and their keyboard enhancer Superkey as a pair, although Sidekick and ProKey get along with no apparent difficulty. If you can, try before you buy any other combination.

Further complication lurks nearby. Because memory capacity has become larger and cheaper, everybody takes advantage of it. Programs tend to grow with each new release as if an immutable corollary to Parkinson's Law were in force. Those called from disk as needed are generally no problem, but memory-resident programs can be. They too are getting larger. Sidekick and Superkey together, for instance, occupy around 100K. By the time you load these programs in addition to DOS, set up a RAM disk of say 160K, and allow for working space, you not only are well into a memory expansion board but may be pushing its limit also. A look at requirements and some planning beforehand can help you avoid unpleasant surprises.

While integrating independent programs to form useful systems currently has many practical limitations, it is a natural extension of the environment created by keyboard enhancers and utilities using window techniques. Given its potential appeal to users if the implementation itself doesn't become too cumbersome, future elaborations seem likely.

Figure 8-1. Example Command Reference Card (Front Side)

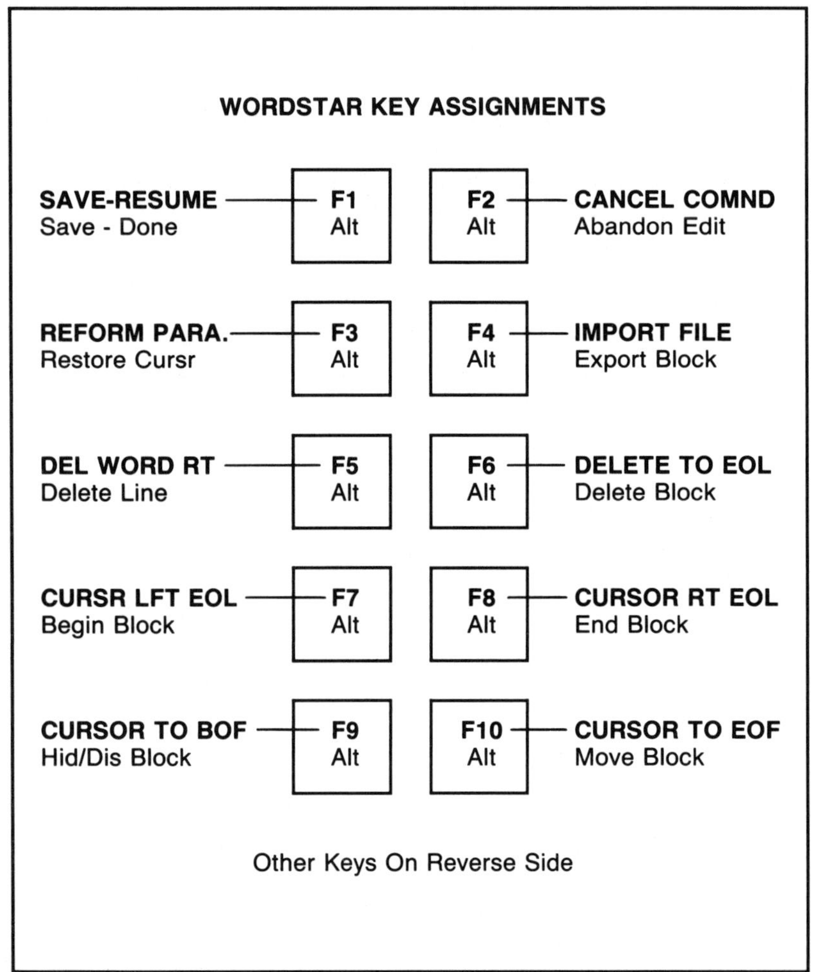

Figure 8-2. Example Command Reference Card (Reverse Side)

WORDSTAR-PROKEY ASSIGNMENTS

Function	ProKey	WS-Key	On-Scr
Bold begin/end	Alt B	^PB	^B
Center line	Alt C	^OC	
Cursor: word right	^→	^F	
Cursor: word left	^←	^A	
Dblstrike prnt b/e	Alt D	^PD	^D
Justify on/off	Alt J	^OJ	
Margin release	Alt M	^OX	
Margin, set L @ -	Alt L	^OL,Esc	
Margin, set R @ -	Alt R	^OR,Esc	
Non-break space	Alt O	^PO	^O
Paragraph indent	Alt I	^OG	
Pitch 10	Alt N	^PN	^N
Pitch 12 (default)	Alt A	^PA	^A
Print cmnd dis/hid	Alt U	^OD	
Printing pause	Alt P	^PC	^C
Repeat next cmnd	Alt Q	^QQ	
Save/Resume @ BOF	Alt K	^KS	
Search and Replace			
Find String	Alt F	^QF	
Find/Rpl again	Alt G	^L	
Find & Replace	Alt H	^QA	
Strikeout beg/end	Alt X	^PX	^X
Subscript beg/end	Alt V	^PV	^V
Superscript b/e	Alt T	^PT	^T
Underline beg/end	Alt S	^PS	^S

Figure 8-3. ProKey Definitions For Preceding Examples

```
<alt=> <altf1> <ctrlk>d<alt->
*
<alt=> <altf2> <ctrlk>q<alt->
*
<alt=> <altf3> <ctrlq>p<alt->
*
<alt=> <altf4> <ctrlk>w<alt->
*
<alt=> <altf5> <ctrly> <alt->
*
<alt=> <altf6> <ctrlk>y<alt->
*
<alt=> <altf7> <ctrlk>b<alt->
*
<alt=> <altf8> <ctrlk>k<alt->
*
<alt=> <altf9> <ctrlk>h<alt->
*
<alt=> <altf10> <ctrlk>v<alt->
*
<alt=> <^rgt> <ctrlf> <alt->
*
<alt=> <^lft> <ctrla> <alt->
*
<alt=> <alta> <ctrlp>a<alt->
*
<alt=> <altb> <ctrlp>b<alt->
*
<alt=> <altc> <ctrlo>c<alt->
*
<alt=> <altd> <ctrlp>d<alt->
*
<alt=> <altf> <ctrlq>f<alt->
*
<alt=> <altg> <ctrll> <alt->
<alt=> <alth> <ctrlq>a<alt->
*
<alt=> <alti> <ctrlo>g<alt->
*
<alt=> <altj> <ctrlo>j<alt->
*
<alt=> <altk> <ctrlk>s<alt->
*
<alt=> <altl> <ctrlo>l<esc> <alt->
*
<alt=> <altm> <ctrlo>x<alt->
*
<alt=> <altn> <ctrlp>n<alt->
*
<alt=> <alto> <ctrlp>o<alt->
*
<alt=> <altp> <ctrlp>c<alt->
*
<alt=> <altq> <ctrlq>q<alt->
*
<alt=> <altr> <ctrlo>r<esc> <alt->
*
<alt=> <alts> <ctrlp>s<alt->
*
<alt=> <altt> <ctrlp>t<alt->
*
<alt=> <altu> <ctrlo>d<alt->
*
<alt=> <altv> <ctrlp>v<alt->
*
<alt=> <altx> <ctrlp>x<alt->
*
<alt=> <alt1>r a:chkdsk<enter> <alt->
*
File updated 10-09-84
```

Note: Above examples are shown in two columns to save space.
Use a single, continuous column for an actual file.

Figure 8-4. Example Of WordStar Customization Records

Addr	*Function*	*Std-Val*	*Mod-Val*	*Result*
(Patches to WS.COM)				
2D0	Med-short Delay	04	01	Cursor blink ratio
2D1	Med-long Delay	08	08	Slower menu rolldown
2D2	Long Delay	10	01	Faster msgs & scr rewrite
2D3	Redisplay Delay	09	01	Faster scr rewrite
360	Help Level	03	02	Dflt to level 2
37B	Char Pitch	00	FF	Dflt to alt (12 cpi)
37E	Page Offset	08	0C	Incr pntd left marg to 12
380	Right Margin	40	4B	Dflt from col 65 to 76
386	Justification	FF	00	Dflt to off
3CD	Pause between pgs	00	FF	Dflt to on
3D3	Omit page numbers	00	FF	Dflt to yes (use .HE)
670	Function Key F1		04,0B,53,11,43	Save-Resume EOF (^KS^QC)
679	Function Key F2		01,15	Cancel command (^U)
682	Function Key F3		01,02	Reform paragraph (^B)
68B	Function Key F4		02,0B,52	Import file (^KR)
694	Function Key F5		01,14	Delete word right (^T)
69D	Function Key F6		02,11,59	Delete to EOL (^QY)
6A6	Function Key F7		02,11,53	Cursor to left EOL (^QS)
6AF	Function Key F8		02,11,44	Cursor to right EOL (^QD)
6B8	Function Key F9		02,11,52	Cursor to BOF (^QR)
6C1	Function Key F10		02,11,43	Cursor to EOF (^QC)
(Patch to WS.COM to enable use of RAM disk as Drive C, version 3.24)				
02DB	Disk reset	from 00	to ff	Prohibit disk reset
02DC	Default Drive	01	03	WS programs on drive C
1E04	B1	90		Enable default drive chg
1E05		01	90	" " " "
(Patches to WSMSGS.OVR)				
3060	Disk File Output Y/N		CE	Highlights dflt value (N)
308F	Use Form Feeds Y/N		CE	" " " (N)
30B3	Suppress Pg Format Y/N		CE	" " " (N)
30E1	Pause Between Pages Y/N		D9	" " " (Y)
(Patches to WSOVLY1.OVR)				
4355,6	Insert On		CF,CE	Highlights word "ON"

9

GETTING THE MOST FROM YOUR PRINTER

Printers are exciting, frustrating, and challenging, especially when the time comes to make them work coherently with an application program. The excitement springs from broad and growing choices available, and the steady erosion of prices under the pressures of competition and advancing technology. These trends encourage upgrades, so questions about how to link new printers with WordStar will continue to arise. Even if you don't plan to upgrade, it is often possible to get more performance from your present printer than is provided by a standard installation.

Improved matrix printers are beginning to threaten the dominance of daisy-wheel printers for high quality printing, and manufacturers of ink-jet printers may yet find a way to combine speed with quality at competitive prices. Most exciting, however, are the evolving laser printers, which may ultimately send all other types except low-cost draft printers into eclipse. Laser printers hold the promise of phototypesetting flexibility and quality which even the best of current letter-quality printers can only approach. Their prices are now about double those of top line daisy-wheel printers, but these prices are beginning to erode, and if past trends prevail, the premium will not last long.

The frustration begins when you discover that the super printer you've been eyeing with racing pulse is not supported by your program. WordStar is about average in the number of printers it supports, meaning that the list includes several popular printers and leaves out a host of others, many of which are worthy of serious consideration. The difference is that, unlike some otherwise good word processors, it is not difficult to tailor WordStar to drive most if not all of them.

All this brings us to the challenging part. Although the means are present in WordStar to drive a great variety of printers and to extract full performance from them, doing so requires moderate study and effort on your part. You can bypass this, of course, by choosing a printer supported by the installation program, but a different model might meet your needs more closely or be a better value. Moreover, standard installation routines seldom implement all the features a printer offers, so even if you use a supported printer, you can benefit from techniques described here.

The required effort is mitigated by a gradual industry trend toward reducing the variety of interface requirements. In several cases you can install an unsupported printer by using the routine for a similar supported model followed by some fine tuning. But for maximum flexibility of choice, you should be acquainted with WordStar's many printer interface functions and understand in general what they do. Although they may seem confusing at first, they fall into logical patterns as you work with them. Understanding them will put you in charge of printer selection and implementation.

Your printer manual must provide adequate information, including a full list of specifications. In particular it should include control codes for all software controllable printer functions and descriptions of what they do and how they are used. Many do, but the details are too often sketchy. If you are considering the purchase of a new printer, it is worth bearing in mind that the quality and completeness of the manual may be an indicator of the manufacturer's attitude toward quality in general.

Finally, all this has the blessing of being a one-time exercise. Once you have gone through it and your printer is doing all the neat tricks it is capable of doing, you can forget it—that is until you succumb to a fever for the latest wonder of printing technology.

WHAT TYPE OF PRINTER TO USE

Although WordStar will work with any type of printer compatible with the IBM PC and similar computers, it requires a microspacing printer to take advantage of the full complement of WordStar page formatting and printing features. What is a microspacing printer? Basically, it is one capable of moving the print head horizontally in increments of 1/120th or 1/60th of an inch and of rolling the platen in 48ths under software command. In the past this ability has been limited to daisy-wheel printers, but matrix printers with this feature, such as the Texas Instruments model 855, have begun to appear. Regardless of the printer type you use, microspacing capability is the key to being able to use such important features as microjustification, proportional spacing, and highly versatile dot commands including those for variable lines per inch and variable pitch. Most dot matrix printers do not have this ability. As to the question of serial versus parallel, it doesn't make a great deal of difference in performance, but you will usually find installation easier and less complex if you choose parallel. Your choice may also be influenced by your present computer equipment configuration and whether you have a serial port, a parallel printer port, or both.

Buying a daisy-wheel printer does not automatically mean that you have microspacing capability. Several of the more inexpensive models on the market do not. If the sales literature does not specify whether a given model has microspacing capability, check the manual for Horizontal Motion Index (HMI) and Vertical Motion Index (VMI) codes. If they are not present, it's a safe bet that the feature is not included.

Selecting printers that take full advantage of WordStar's features and applying the details presented later will be easier if you are familiar with printer basics. The next two sections are included for that purpose.

UNDERSTANDING PRINTER INTERFACES

Itself an often carelessly applied bit of jargon, the term interface as used here refers to the interconnection—electrical or functional—between printer and processor or between printer and software. For proper operation these interfaces must be compatible; therefore, specifications and certain operating ground rules apply. Unless you already have a working knowledge of printers, much of the information in back sections of your printer manual may seem confusing since, if comprehensive, it deals with more than just the software interface. The following will help you sort it out.

Two kinds of interfaces are involved. First is the machine interface between printer and processor. It is primarily electrical, thus involving the hardware, but as we will see shortly, it also has a functional aspect which, in the IBM PC, involves DOS. Second is the program interface between WordStar and the printer. It relates primarily to operating controls and functional commands used in actual printing, such as carriage returns, line feeds, changes of pitch, boldfacing, underlining, and so forth.

The machine interface and related specifications have to do with the physical wiring connections and the basic method by which the processor and printer communicate with each other. The latter is called a protocol, also known as the "handshaking" interface. It specifies how data is transferred to the printer, how the printer signals it is ready or not ready to receive data, how faults are reported, and the like. You might think of all this as being analogous to the functions performed by DOS for application programs. That is, it creates an operating environment in which useful work—in this case printing—can be done. Its purpose is not only to standardize that environment but to improve the efficiency of application programs by taking care of essential housekeeping tasks.

Two types of hardware interfaces are used with personal computers, serial and parallel. The serial interface is known as such because data bits are transmitted to the printer one after the other, or serially. The most common serial protocol is one established by the Electronic Industries Association and is known as RS-232C. One of its appeals is that wiring is simplified, requiring only six to eight wires in most cases. As you would expect, the parallel interface transfers data bits in parallel, a full byte at a time. The most common parallel interface and protocol were popularized by Centronics, a manufacturer of printers. While this interface does not have official industry backing, it is a defacto standard. Wiring for the Centronics interface is more complex, involving up to 36 wires, but from a software viewpoint, it is simpler. Parallel also has a theoretical edge over serial in terms of data transfer rate, but practically speaking, the printer itself determines printing speed.

To place all this in perspective, consider the functional block diagram shown in figure 9-1. You might think of WordStar, DOS, the processor, and your printer as waypoints along a communication highway. The main lane of this highway, which we'll call the command and data lane, connects WordStar to the printer. Between each succeeding pair of waypoints, other functions are added to support the main highway. These also serve as auxiliary lanes in the sense that they sometimes provide for special communications between connected blocks. For instance, fault interrupts such as out-of-paper or end-of-ribbon signals from the printer are handled by the operating system. As long as the main highway remains intact, intermediate points are in effect transparent to WordStar, and it "sees" the printer directly.

Figure 9-1. WordStar, System, And Printer Interfaces

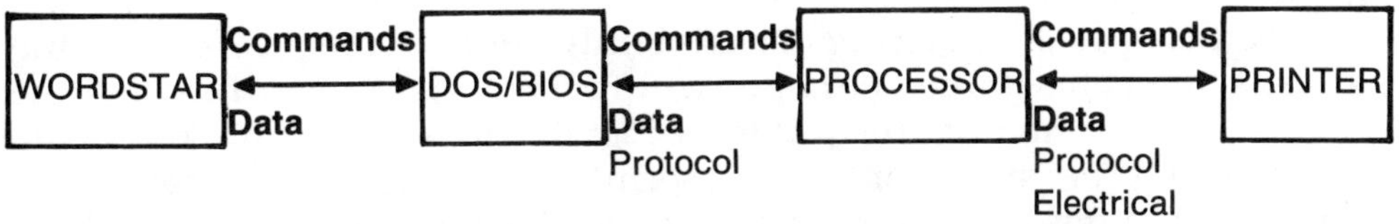

WORDSTAR ⟷ Commands / Data ⟷ DOS/BIOS ⟷ Commands / Data / Protocol ⟷ PROCESSOR ⟷ Commands / Data / Protocol / Electrical ⟷ PRINTER

A FEW PRINTER FUNDAMENTALS

Printer manufacturers have taken advantage of advances in microcircuit technology to build-in data storage capability and expanded control logic, increasing the number of available features and making printers much more productive. An example is bidirectional printing. Returning the print head to its home position for each new line involves wasted motion and lost time. Therefore, modern printers print a line from left to right, advance the paper without a carriage return, and print the next line from right to left. This requires a "look ahead" function, either built into the printer or in the program, to determine where to begin lines printed backward so that left margins stay aligned. A temporary data storage area, called a buffer, is often included for this purpose or simply to reduce the frequency of program interrupts by the printer to request more print data. Ribbon color changes, switches in type style, and programmable accessories like sheet feeders are increasingly common. Such features increase versatility, but they also complicate the interface between program and printer. We must inform the program, in WordStar's case with appropriate table entries, about available printer features and how to invoke them.

Although the ultimate purpose of all printers is to convert encoded signals sent by the program into printed images on paper, the way they do this varies considerably with the type and make of printer. Matrix printers use a print head employing fine, hardened wires that are perpendicular to the platen to create an image on paper in the form of small dots. Very small electric solenoids "fire" these wires in a pattern determined by the character to be printed, causing them to move rapidly forward and strike the ribbon to produce printed images. Since the wires are extremely light in weight and are always in position, relatively high printing speeds can be achieved, but the dots of which characters are formed can be readily seen. To provide higher resolution in printed characters, manufacturers have done two things—increase the number of wires and make them finer, and provide for more than one printing pass to fill in the gaps. The latter improves quality at the expense of speed.

Because printed images are synthesized from individual dots, different character sets or print enhancements such as boldface, italics, and expanded or compressed type styles can be built into matrix printers. Usually this is done by storing in a read-only memory the print-wire firing patterns for each set and character within a set. Again, we must tell the program what commands the printer recognizes to select them. Controlling selection of type styles on matrix printers is a good application for information in this chapter, because standard Install routines ignore these capabilities.

Daisy-wheel printers differ in several ways. First, of course, they print fully-formed characters which are molded into the ends of petals on the print wheel or thimble. They do this by rotating the print wheel so that a selected character is aligned in printing position between a solenoid and the ribbon. The solenoid is then fired, and a plunger strikes the back of the petal driving it forward to compress petal and ribbon against the paper, transferring an inked image to paper. The need to rotate the print wheel, and practical limitations on how fast that can be done, is why these printers are inherently slower than matrix printers. In operation, a daisy printer converts character codes received from the program into print-wheel positioning information. It prints whatever is physically present at these selected positions; therefore, what characters are actually printed depends on the character arrangement of the print wheel.

Daisy printers with microspacing ability produce print enhancements by a different scheme than is used by matrix printers. Horizontal movement of the print head or carriage is controlled by a function called horizontal motion index (HMI). This tells the printer how far to move the print head before printing the next character. The range of motion possible is from zero to a large fraction of an inch or more, depending on the printer. Boldface printing is done by double-striking a character with a small print head movement between strikes, usually 1/120-inch but sometimes 1/60-inch. Underlining and overprinting, or other operations requiring a double pass with most matrix printers, are done by printing two characters in sequence with no intervening print head movement. Actual HMI values are sent to the printer by WordStar; they are related to width values described in Chapter 10 and to the in-text print format command being executed.

Paper feed for operations involving vertical movement, up or down, is controlled by vertical motion index (VMI). For most printers it is specified in increments of 1/48-inch. Non-microspacing printers can also provide for vertical movement, such as that needed to print subscripts and superscripts, but this involves a different set of WordStar printer controls.

THE BASIC WORDSTAR-TO-PRINTER INTERFACE

Having examined system interfaces and basic printer characteristics, we now consider how WordStar communicates with the printer. The commands you use in text to signify boldface, underlining, line height, and so on are not the actual commands WordStar issues to the printer. It wouldn't understand them in that form. The program interprets these commands as it reads a text file and converts them to a form usable by the printer. These translations come from entries in WS.COM which, for supported printers, are supplied by the Install program. For unsupported printers we will make these entries based on printer instruction book data.

If all printers recognized the same set of command codes, life would be much simpler since one set of translations would serve for all. Unhappily, this is not the case. Basic commands, such as those for carriage returns, line feeds, and backspacing, have become fairly well standardized. This is why you can install nearly any printer as either what WordStar refers to as a standard printer or a backspacing standard printer, and it will at least put characters on paper. Access to advanced features, however, is another matter. Codes for given features often differ from one manufacturer to another, and the more crammed a printer is with features, the more likely it is to use unique and sometimes elaborate codes.

Since command codes vary in form and length, WordStar includes generous table space for them. You will find that space allocations are not the same for all functions, with more space provided for commands that potentially are longer and more complex. Also included is unassigned space for four user-definable functions (accessed by ^PQ, ^PW, ^PE, and ^PR commands in text). These are useful for control of features like expanded and condensed printing on matrix printers, or for controlling accessories such as sheet feeders on daisy printers.

Not all of WordStar's printer commands are visible in the sense of having equivalent keyboard commands. Many are generated internally, based on entries we or the Install program have made. Examples are the various horizontal and vertical motion controls related to microspacing printers. Others are the lead-in string that sets up initial printer conditions when you start printing and the finishing string sent when a job is complete.

WORDSTAR'S PRINTER FUNCTIONS AND COMMANDS

This section describes command characters and sequences WordStar sends to your printer to establish proper basic operation and to invoke specific print commands. Some of the entries described here, such as POSMTH, are not to control the printer directly but to inform WordStar about major printer characteristics which influence the operating interface. Terms used in your printer manual may differ slightly from one manufacturer to another and from those used here, so emphasis at this point is on the functions involved.

At the end of this chapter are address listings and related information for each function. Corresponding descriptions and application notes are presented here. Each command or function is listed by name, followed by its label. These descriptions are in order of their appearance in memory. They are not always grouped according to their applicability to microspacing or non-microspacing printers, so be sure to check the notes carefully before using the information.

In general, the formats of required entries follow the practices used elsewhere in WordStar. Many commands or data entries are only a single byte long. Other fields are multiple bytes in length to accommodate varying lengths of entries required for different printers. In such cases the first byte in the field must be a length byte indicating the number of characters in the following command string. (If it is zero, the function is disabled.)

Printer Overstrike Method (POSMTH) This parameter is very important since it specifies to WordStar what type of printer is connected: non-backspacing, backspacing, or microspacing, thus determining what print features are available and how they are implemented.

FF Designates a printer that produces print enhancements, such as bold or underlining, by overprinting complete lines. It can return the carriage without line feed but has no backspacing ability. Applies to most dot matrix printers.

00 Printer can overprint by returning carriage without line feed or by backspacing. Normal overstriking will be done by backspacing except for overprinted lines ^P Ret). Applies mostly to daisy wheel printers without microspacing.

01 Microspacing printer capable of horizontal motion increments in 120ths or 60ths and vertical motion in 48ths. Provides for fullest use of WordStar print features.

Boldface Strikes (BLDSTR) Specifies number of strikes for boldface print, normally 2. Can be increased for non-microspacing printers to produce darker images at the expense of print speed. Do not change for microspacing printers, since the microspacing algorithm is not set up for more than two strikes. (However, you can combine boldface and double strike commands in text, i.e. ^PB^PD, for increased emphasis.) Applies to all values of POSMTH.

Double-Strike Printing (DBLSTR) Specifies number of strikes for increased emphasis, normally set to 2. Can be increased as desired for microspacing and non-microspacing printers, but reduces effective print speed.

Carriage Return and Line Feed (PSCRLF) Control characters for CR and LF sent when Returns are encountered in text files. Normally it does not apply to microspacing printers (POSMTH = 1). If yours is one of the diminishing number of printers that automatically line feed on a carriage return, remove the LF character (0A). It is better, however, to disable the auto line feed at the printer if possible. Applies for POSMTH values of FF and 01.

Carriage Return (PSCR) Returns carriage to beginning of line without line feed; for overprinting, underline, double strike, and when in-text backspace is encountered. Applies when POSMTH is FF and, for overprint commands only, when POSMTH is 00.

Carriage Return and Half Line Feed (PSHALF) A holdover from days when some printers, such as converted Selectrics, did half-line feeds. Can be used in conjunction with preceding command to do subscripts and superscripts at half-line intervals. Applies when POSMTH is FF or 00.

Backspace Command (PBACKS) Used for underline, double strike, and other applications when ^H is encountered in text. Applies when POSMTH is 00.

Alternate Pitch (PALT) Enter command to set printer to alternate pitch (12, 15 cpi, etc.) if available. On wide pitches, remember that maximum column width displayable on monitor without horizontal scrolling (76 columns) limits printed column width. Applies for POSMTH values FF and

00. Access from text with ^PA. (Note: microspacing printers implement pitch changes indirectly by appropriate HMI values sent by WordStar. See page formatting section in Chapter 6. With these printers you can use either ^PA or .CW commands for pitch changes.)

Standard Pitch (PSTD) Enter command to return printer to standard pitch. Applies to POSMTH values FF and 00. Access with ^PN. (See preceding note.)

Sub/Superscript Roll (ROLUP) Enter command to roll paper back a partial line before printing a superscript and after a subscript. Be sure to enter related command for rolling paper forward. Applies when POSMTH is FF or 00.

Sub/Superscript Roll (ROLDOW) Complements preceding command. Also applies when POSMTH is FF or 00. (Microspacing printers do these operations through appropriate vertical motion index values sent by WordStar.)

User-Defined Functions (USR1 - USR4) These fields provide for up to four user-selected printer control functions. Each field includes a length byte and space for up to four control characters. Printer control functions you install here are accessed by ^PQ, ^PW, ^PE, and ^PR, respectively, entered in text. These are useful for implementing printer functions not otherwise accessible by WordStar commands. Examples, some described later, include switches of type style or print mode—as from draft to letter-quality or correspondence mode—and control of accessories such as sheet feeders. Text lines containing these commands always print in forward direction. Applies for all POSMTH values.

Alternate Ribbon Color (RIBBON) Enter control characters to switch ribbon colors on printers so equipped. This function and its following complement are invoked by ^PY commands embedded in text and act as toggles: the first ^PY command invokes RIBBON and the second invokes RIBOFF. The pair can also be used for any other toggled function, such as turning a special type face on and off, if your printer does not have an alternate ribbon color. In this case you may wish to alter the print menu to reflect the change (see Chapter 5). Applicable to all POSMTH values.

Return To Standard Ribbon Color (RIBOFF) Complement to above.

Printer Initialization (PSINIT) This sequence is sent by WordStar when you start printing a file. Enter characters specified in the printer manual to set your printer to its ready-to-print state. At a minimum this should be a carriage return to put the print head in its home position. You may also want to include commands to clear its buffer, etc. With some printers the power-up sequence when you turn the printer on does this automatically, but if you leave power on between jobs, you may want to include an appropriate sequence anyway—it all depends on how you use your printer. Applicable to all values of POSMTH.

Printing Job Finish (PSFINI) This sequence is sent by WordStar when a file is finished printing. Again, if you leave power on between printing jobs you will need an appropriate string to ready the printer for the next job. Whether you need this in PSINIT or PSFINI depends on your printer; some may require operations such as clearing a print buffer at the start, and others may require them at the end. Generally it does no particular harm to have a similar or duplicate string in both. If your printer is equipped with a bell, you might want to include its command (usually 07h) to provide an audible signal at the end of a printing job. Applies to all POSMTH values.

Strike-Out Character (SOCHR) This is the character which overprints when you invoke a ^PX command. Normally a hyphen (2Dh), you can change it to any other character of your choice, for instance a slash (2Fh). Applicable to all values of POSMTH.

Underline Character (ULCHR) This is the character overprinted when you invoke a ^PS command. Applicable to all values of POSMTH.

Printer Driver (CSWTCH) This is a one-byte entry that specifies which of several available internal program routines are used to send characters from WordStar to the printer. Only two apply to the IBM PC and similar machines using PC-DOS/MS-DOS: a value of 00 is used for a parallel printer, and 04 is used for a serial printer. Applicable to all values of POSMTH. (Note: When a serial printer is used, the DOS Mode command must be used as explained later in this chapter.)

Busy Routine (HAVBSY) A one-byte entry indicating when a separate routine is used to signal a "printer-busy" status. Should always be 00 for PC.

Protocol (PROTCL) A one-byte entry denoting whether a special "printer buffer full" routine is used and, if so, of what type. WordStar supports ETX/ACK (PROTCL=01) and XON/XOFF (PROTCL=02) protocols for serial printers if your printer is so equipped. (These are discussed further in the section on serial printers.) None is used in the IBM PC and compatible systems for parallel printers, and the correct entry in this case is 00.

Buffer Size (EAKBSZ) Enter half the size of your printer's buffer here. (WordStar in effect uses the halves separately.) Applies only if you use a serial printer and have implemented ETX/ACK protocol (PROTCL=01). Defaults to 127 (7Fh). Applicable to all values of POSMTH.

VMI Lead-in String (DVMILE) String that enables vertical motion index values to be accepted by microspacing printers. Applies only when POSMTH is 01. Defaults to Esc RS (1B 1E in hex), a sequence used by many Diablo and Qume printers, and others which emulate these.

VMI Trailer String (DVMITR) Vertical motion index trailer sequence, sent after the VMI value is transmitted. Not often used except by the NEC 3550. Applies only when POSMTH is 01. (Not present before version 3.3.)

Minimum VMI Value (DVMMIN) Specifies the minimum value of vertical motion index recognized by the printer (for zero motion). For many Diablo, Qume, and related printers it is 1. For other printers it can be 0. If your printer has a built-in "bias" or offset, it can be greater; check the manual carefully. Applies only when POSMTH is 01.

Vertical Motion Range (DVMRNG) Specifies range of vertical motion increments your printer will accept, plus 1. The value you enter is 1 higher than the maximum specified in your printer manual. Defaults to 126 (7Eh), a common value for Diablo and Qume printers. For NEC printers it is usually less. Applies only when POSMTH is 01. (Note: DVMMIN plus DVMRNG cannot exceed 255; see note at DHRNG.)

HMI Lead-in String (DHMILE) Enables horizontal motion index values to be accepted by your printer. Defaults to Esc US (1B 1F in hex), a commonly used sequence. Applies only when POSMTH is 01.

HMI Flag (DHMIFG) Normally 00 for printers which space horizontally in 120ths of an inch. If your printer is capable of spacing in 60ths only, change to FF. Applies only when POSMTH is 01.

Minimum HMI Value (DHMIN) Specifies the minimum value of horizontal motion index recognized by the printer (for zero motion). Defaults to 01, a common value for Diablo and Qume printers. Again, your printer may have a built-in bias or offset requiring this value to be higher; check the manual. Applies only when POSMTH is 01.

Horizontal Motion Range (DHRNG) Specifies range of horizontal motion increments your printer will accept, plus 1. Add 1 to the value specified in your manual. Applies only when POSMTH is 01. (Note: The total value of DHMIN plus DHRNG cannot exceed 255. If it does, reduce DHRNG to bring the total within this limit. This reduces the maximum HMI value available, but it will still be much larger than normally needed.)

Forward Printing (DFWD) Sequence to print a line in forward direction. Defaults to Esc 5 (1B 35 in hex). Applies only when POSMTH is 01.

Backward Printing (DBAK) Sequence to print a line in reverse direction. Defaults to Esc 6 (1B 36 in hex). Applies only when POSMTH is 01. This and the preceding sequence provide for bidirectional printing.

Forward Space (DSP) Normally the ASCII space character (20h). Applies only when POSMTH is 01.

Backspace (DBS) Normally the ASCII backspace character (08h). Applies only when POSMTH is 01.

Line Feed (DLF) Normally the ASCII line-feed character (0Ah). Applies only when POSMTH is 01.

Reverse Line Feed (DRLF) Sequence to reverse paper feed one line, often Esc LF (1B 0A in hex). Applies only when POSMTH is 01.

Print Phantom Space (DPHSPC) This and the next sequence can be used, on printers so equipped, to print non-ASCII characters that may be present on a print wheel. Cents and degree signs are examples. Diablo and Qume printers often have this feature, but others may not. Defaults to Esc Y (1B 59 in hex). Access with ^PF in text. Applies only when POSMTH is 01.

Print Phantom Rubout (DPHRUB) See the above comments. Defaults to Esc Z (1B 5A in hex). Access with ^PG in text. Applies only when POSMTH is 01.

PRACTICAL UNSUPPORTED PRINTER INSTALLATION

As mentioned earlier, a practical way to begin the installation of an unsupported printer is to run the Install program for a similar type or make of supported printer. (Note: Installation programs supplied with various releases of WordStar have different names; in version 3.3, for instance, it is WINSTALL.COM. The more general name Install used here applies to all.) Install programs and WordStar manuals don't tell you much about identifying printer types. They use the vague term "specialty" or "letter-quality" to refer to a microspacing printer, in the past meaning only a daisy or thimble printer. If you start with a supported model from the same manufacturer, be sure the general characteristics are the same. Manufacturers frequently offer different types of printers to round out their product lines. Sales literature, the printer manual, or your dealer can often help you determine if the printer you wish to install is functionally similar to another.

Prior to version 3.3 you had only one choice of dot matrix printer, the IBM parallel, which is an Epson MX-80 with IBM label and slightly modified command set. With version 3.3 other matrix printers were added, including the NEC 8023A, the Okidata ML84A, and the TI 810. Any of these are suitable for a start-up or prototype installation for a matrix printer, since basic installation routines provided for them in WordStar are identical. These routines are cleaner than the default IBM parallel printer routine in that unused functions are more thoroughly nulled out.

Many microspacing daisy-wheel printers emulate Diablo commands, so you can often use a basic Diablo 630 as your baseline if you are installing a microspacing printer. The parameters for several Qume printers are similar to the 630, but those for NEC printers are different. Installation for a microspacing printer is more complex than that for a matrix printer, because even the basic process involves numerous parameters relating to horizontal and vertical motions. You may find it helpful to read parts dealing with these functions in the section on microspacing printers.

As you run the Install program for the printer you have selected as a prototype, you will of course be prompted to indicate parallel or serial interface and choice of protocol. The latter applies only if you are using a serial interface, and it may be best to indicate no protocol at first to simplify the basic installation. To complete the installation you may also find helpful the section on serial printers later in this chapter. Some printers offer a selectable choice of serial or parallel interface; it will almost always simplify the process if you choose parallel.

Once you have run the Install program for the prototype, it is a good idea to make a printed dump of the area within WS.COM containing entries for printers. This area is the three memory blocks displayed by successive D commands in Debug, beginning at address 0740 and ending with 08BF. (If you don't recall how to do this, refer to Chapter 2. If you have already made a program dump as suggested there, use that.) Then referring to the address and functional listings in table 9-1 at the end of this chapter, go through the printout and circle the entries for each function, beginning with POSMTH and ending with DPHRUB. Note that some of the entries will appear to start one byte later than they should; this is because their length bytes have been zeroed by Install for parameters that are irrelevant to the type of printer you have selected. It may also be helpful to write in the labels on your printout. Throughout this and following operations, proceed carefully and double-check your work to avoid later frustration due to errors.

You will now have a detailed picture of the complete WordStar-printer interface, from which you can learn a good deal. First, several entries are not relevant to your type of printer. That is, entries are present for both matrix and daisy-wheel printers. The reason is that the set of parameters from which a specific installation is extracted by Install contains default values for both types. They are modified as needed or simply ignored if the selected value of POSMTH makes them irrelevant. As a general rule, unneeded entries that do not have an associated length byte are nullified by giving them values of FF. Multibyte entries are nulled by setting the length byte to zero. How do you know which entries are needed and which are not? Refer back to the preceding section describing printer functions. The POSMTH value, determined by the type of printer you have, in turn determines which functions apply—as noted in the descriptions.

You will also note that many functions, including PALT, PSTD, ROLUP, ROLDOW, USR1 through USR4, and so forth are not implemented. Many of these apply only to dot matrix and other non-microspacing printers, since many print enhancements are inherently enabled in microspacing printers by their incremental horizontal and vertical motion capabilities. Standard WordStar installation routines for all printers are basic in the sense that they implement few special features. We will provide redress later, but for now we will focus on basic installation.

With a printout of your baseline or prototype printer installation and the control codes listed in your printer instruction manual, you should be able to determine readily which entries will need to be modified. You will find that many of these entries are Escape codes; that is, an ASCII Escape (hex 1B) followed by one or more numbers or characters. For the present, concentrate on determining the correct values for PSINIT, PSFINI, POSMTH, and CSWTCH. For a daisy or other microspacing printer, you should also check values for all functions whose labels begin with D, especially DVMILE, DVMMIN, DVMRNG, DHMILE, DHMIN, DHRNG, DFWD, and DBAK. These labels are of course unique to WordStar, and they will not appear in your printer manual. You will have to correlate labels with functions by their descriptions.

All this may seem like a complex undertaking, but it is not difficult as long as you use a systematic approach. It is recommended that you set up a worksheet as illustrated in figure 9-2 with column headings as shown there in bold. These headings are followed by several typical entries, the first eight of which apply to printers of all types. Addresses are for version 3.3; check and change them as required for earlier versions. Actual values listed to the right are for example only. Yours may be different.

Begin by entering on your worksheet the addresses and labels for each function required for your basic installation. Then, by examining either an on-screen dump or the printout you previously made, determine and enter on the worksheet the present values for each function. These values are the ones made by Install for the printer you picked as a prototype. Values for functions that inform WordStar of the type of printer and interface (POSMTH and CSWTCH) should not need to be changed if you chose a good prototype, nor should standard commands and characters such as carriage returns, line feeds, backspaces, and the underline and strikeout characters.

Now refer to your printer manual to determine control codes or values for each function unique to your printer, and enter these on the worksheet. If you are installing a matrix printer, these normally will be only PSINIT and PSFINI at this point. For a microspacing printer you will also need

Figure 9-2. Sample Worksheet For Unsupported Printer Installation

Address	Label	Present-Value	Req'd-ASCII	Lgth	Hex-Equiv
0746	POSMTH	(FF, 00, or 01)	(note 1)	——(2)	(enter value)
0747	BLDSTR	02	02	——	02
0748	DBLSTR	02	02	——	02
.	.	.	.	.	.
.	.	.	.	.	.
079D	PSINIT	01 0D	Esc CR P	03	1B 0D 50
07AE	PSFINI	01 0D	CR Esc CR P	04	0D 1B 0D 50
07C1	ULCHR	2D	_	——	2D
07C2	SOCHR	5F	-	——	5F
07C9	CSWTCH	(01 or 04)	(note 1)	——	(enter value)
(Following examples apply only if POSMTH = 01, microspacing printer)					
088A	DHMILE	02 1B 1F	Esc]	02	1B 5D
0890	DHMIN	01	@	——	40
0892	DHRNG	7E	15 + 1	——	10

Notes: 1) Values determined by printer type and interface selected (P or S).
2) Double dash indicates no length byte required for this entry.

entries for all labeled functions beginning with D, and to figure out some of these it may be necessary to refer to the section of this chapter dealing with special microspacing printer considerations. At a minimum, the printer manual should contain the ASCII codes; enter these under the appropriate worksheet heading. Some manuals also list hex equivalents; if not included, look them up in Appendix A and enter them as shown. Finally, enter a length value if needed, which is the number of bytes in the Hex-Equiv column. Remember, the requirement for a length byte is not related to how many bytes are present but to how the field is defined in WordStar. In several cases you could need a length byte for a one-byte entry in the Hex-Equiv column. (Requirements for length bytes and other format conventions are included in the listings in table 9-1 at the end of this chapter.)

When you have completed filling out your worksheet, you are ready to begin actually entering the hex values in WS.COM. If you are using version 3.3, you have three options: you can use the patcher, the custom printer installation routine, or Debug. If you are using an earlier version, you are limited to the latter, which is recommended in any event. Again, it would be wise to check your worksheet for accuracy before proceeding.

Once you complete your patches to WS.COM, reload WordStar and print a test file, preferably one containing print enhancements such as boldface, underlining, superscripts, subscripts, and so forth. If you have made only a basic installation for a matrix printer, these enhancements may not print unless you have jumped ahead and made appropriate additional entries, but it should produce straight text indicating that the basic installation is okay. On the other hand, if you installed a microspacing printer, everything in the file should print exactly—but only with luck. More likely, something will not work the first time. If you have been careful, however, your printer should at least put characters on paper, giving you something to analyze for debugging. Failure to print bold, for example, might indicate an error in HMI inputs, while failure to print subscripts or superscripts may point to a problem with VMI inputs. Be sure you entered the right value for POSMTH, in this case 01.

Incorrect switch settings are a common problem, especially on printers with numerous switch-selectable features. If you have difficulty, check all switches on the printer to be sure they are in the right positions before doing anything else. The premise for this is simple: Always do the easiest things first; this can save you a lot of work. In general, switches for automatic line feed, bidirectional printing, and proportional spacing should be off if you are using a microspacing printer; these functions are handled internally by WordStar. If all your debugging efforts fail, try printing from another program. You could have a cabling problem or the wrong set of inputs at PSINIT.

Whatever the printer, once you have verified the basic installation and have the printer operating as it should for that level of implementation, you can start thinking about added features and performance enhancements. First, document your installation so that you can duplicate the process if necessary. From this point on you can experiment with confidence. You know how the basic installation process works, and if you really foul things up, you know how to recover with at least a semblance of grace.

SPECIAL CONSIDERATIONS FOR MICROSPACING PRINTERS

Establishing correct values for the various vertical and horizontal motion parameters can be difficult, partly because certain conventions within WordStar must be observed but mostly because the way these parameters are expressed can vary considerably from one printer to another. Lack of standardization in terminology does not help either. You will sometimes have to hunt for a desired parameter in the printer manual, and it may be called something other than what you expect.

Both vertical and horizontal motion are controlled by four parameters: (1) a lead-in sequence, such as Esc US, (2) a minimum value, which can be zero or some larger value referred to as a bias or offset but still producing zero motion, (3) a range of permissible values, usually expressed as a maximum value from which you must calculate the range if the minimum value specified in your printer manual is greater than zero, and (4) the actual motion value itself, usually represented by a lower-case letter n in printer manuals and sent by WordStar to the printer. The fourth item does not require any action on your part; the program calculates it and sends it automatically. Some printers, notably the NEC 3550, also require a trailer string, or sequence of characters that finish up an operation.

In WordStar the first three parameters are labeled (in order) DVMILE, DVMMIN, and DVMRNG for vertical motion, and DHMILE, DHMIN, and DHRNG for horizontal motion. The vertical motion trailer string for NEC printers is labeled DVMITR but exists in version 3.3 only; prior to that it was handled by a special patch. Collectively these functions are referred to as VMI (vertical motion index) and HMI (horizontal motion index), but this is for convenience only; the actual index values have no table entries.

For many microspacing printers, minimum values for VMI and HMI are 1, but this is not always the case. Sometimes it is zero or some value greater than 1. Referring again to figure 9-2, note in the example for DHMIN that an offset is present; that is, the minimum is expressed as ASCII character @, equivalent to decimal 64. You will need to determine the value for your printer from data in your manual. Vertical and horizontal range values are subject to the WordStar convention of being expressed as the maximum value stated in the printer manual (or calculated from offset values) plus 1. This is also illustrated in figure 9-2 by the example for DHRNG. Finally, once you have determined all required values, usually in decimal, you must remember to convert all these to hexadecimal. These are the values entered in the last column of your worksheet and patched into WS.COM.

The remaining entries for microspacing printers should seldom present problems. The characters used in DSP, DBS, DLF, and usually DRLF as well are more or less standard. Determining the correct values for DFWD and DBAK is mainly a matter of finding them in your printer manual. Provision for printing so-called phantom characters, DPHSPC and DPHRUB, may or may not exist on your printer. If it is a Diablo or Qume emulator, it probably will. This leaves only the ribbon color change feature, RIBBON and RIBOFF, if your printer is so equipped. It, too, involves only looking up the codes and plugging them in at the specified addresses.

SPECIAL CONSIDERATIONS FOR SERIAL PRINTERS

If you wish to install a serial printer, the main parameter change is to CSWTCH, which is automatically modified if you specify a serial interface in the Install routine. PROTCL and EAKBSZ may or may not require attention, depending on whether you select a protocol and, if so, of what type. None of the other parameters are affected unless your particular make of printer makes a distinction between serial and parallel models in the way commands are implemented, which is unlikely.

There is no flat answer as to whether or not using a protocol, and of what type, will produce better results. In general, a protocol will be necessary if your printer is capable of printing at speeds faster than 300 baud (approximately 30 characters per second) and you wish to take full advantage of printer speed. Your printer, of course, first must support a protocol. If it supports both ETX/ACK and XON/XOFF, the latter is probably the better choice, but some experimentation may be in order to verify this. As detailed in the previous section on function descriptions, an appropriate entry is required at EAKBSZ if you use an ETX/ACK protocol; otherwise, it is irrelevant.

If you use a serial printer, it will be necessary to define the PC's serial port parameters with suitable DOS commands and then redirect the line printer function to the communications port. A common way of doing this is to include necessary command lines in an autoexec batch file, normally the same file you use to boot WordStar. You should consult your printer manual to determine parameter values for baud rate, parity, and number of data bits and stop bits. Your DOS manual will explain format requirements under the MODE command section, options 3 and 4. Don't forget that you must include the DOS program MODE.COM on your working WordStar diskette. Typical command lines (before the line invoking WordStar) in your autoexec batch file would appear as follows:

```
mode com1:1200,n,8,1,p
mode lpt1:=com1:
```

The situation gets more complex when you use a print spooler. If you use spooler software or an expansion board from AST Research, details on serial interfaces as well as specifics for implementing their spooler are thoroughly documented in their manual. If you use another type of expansion board or spooler software, check to be sure what protocols are supported.

GETTING MORE PERFORMANCE FROM NON-MICROSPACING PRINTERS

As pointed out earlier, standard WordStar installation routines do little more for a matrix printer than enable it to put characters on paper. However, you need not live with this, as implementing numerous additional features is not hard to do. To illustrate how this is done, we will develop a set of enhancements for a popular matrix printer, the Okidata ML92. (Its companion ML93 is identical except for a longer carriage.) Although the codes may be different for other printers, the principles are the same and apply also to non-microspacing daisy-wheel models.

Matrix printers in general, especially top-of-line models, incorporate almost overwhelming arrays of features. Indeed, printer manufacturers seem to be engaged in a features race, each seeking to outdo its competitors by sheer numbers of features alone. The result, even for sophisticated users, is that a walk through the manual's feature descriptions and control code lists can be an exercise in confusion. Many printers have special graphics modes and features useful in other applications, but of little relevance in word processing. Sorting all this out is a challenge.

Most of these printers have some ability to switch pitches and offer various print enhancements such as compressed, expanded, or double-width type. Many also support the printing of subscripts and superscripts, and several offer a letter-quality or correspondence mode. These we will focus on, using WordStar printer control functions not implemented in the standard installation. Since these functions have already been defined, we will assume you are familiar with what they do and will refer to them by label.

Figure 9-3 illustrates how this can be done for the ML92/93 and, by substituting appropriate codes specified in your printer manual, for other matrix printers. These techniques also apply to non-microspacing daisy printers (POSMTH = 00). For illustration purposes the format shown here is a little different from the worksheet described earlier (figure 9-2), but when actually preparing installation data, it is recommended that you use the worksheet. This procedure also assumes that you have first done a basic installation as previously described. If you are using version 3.3, select the ML84A; for earlier versions use the IBM parallel printer as a baseline.

Since 12 cpi and 10 cpi are the two most commonly used pitches for word processing, and are most consistent with the internal structure of WordStar, it is logical to assign them to PALT and PSTD respectively, although you could choose others available on your printer if desired. If you normally use 12 cpi as your standard pitch, you might be inclined to assign it to PSTD instead of PALT, but a better way to do this is simply to make PALT the default pitch as explained in Chapter 6.

Figure 9-3. Typical Enhanced Functions For An Okidata ML92/93

Function	Lgth	Value(s)	Description	Access
PALT	01	1C	Set pitch to 12 cpi	^PA
PSTD	01	1E	Set pitch to 10 cpi	^PN
ROLUP	02	1B 4A	Superscript On	^PT
ROLDOW	02	1B 4C	Subscript On	^PV
USR1	02	1B 31	Correspondence quality	^PQ
USR2	02	1B 30	Select DP mode	^PW
USR3	01	1B	Wild Card - see text	^PE
USR4	01	1D	Set pitch to 17 cpi	^PR
RIBBON	01	1F	Double-width characters	^PY
RIBOFF	01	1E	Return to 10 cpi	^PY
PSINIT	04	18 0D 1B 30	Clr buf, CR, DP mode	——
PSFINI	04	18 0D 1B 30	same	——

Superscripts and subscripts in non-microspacing printers are controlled by the functions ROLUP and ROLDOW. Their internal operation is different from the way scripting operations are handled for microspacing printers, but in-text commands are the same, and they work the same way. Originally these functions were developed for printers that could roll the platen up or down a partial line but did not use VMI commands to do it. Some matrix printers may not physically roll the platen, but if they use some variation of on-off sequence to initiate and terminate scripting operations, you probably can adapt these functions to the purpose.

Whenever you initiate a superscript command (^PT), the control sequence at ROLUP is sent to the printer. When WordStar encounters the next ^PT in text it sends the sequence at ROLDOW. Operation for subscripts (^PV) is the same except the order is reversed, ROLDOW being sent first. This works for the ML92 since it will terminate scripting upon receipt of a complementary script control sequence. Thus, only two of its four available sequences are needed here, and they fit nicely into ROLUP and ROLDOW. The situation is not as clean with Epson MX/FX-80 printers or those that are Epson emulators. These printers require a separate command (Esc T) to turn scripting off, forcing you to use one of WordStar's USR functions. Assuming you used USR1, your in-text command to end a scripting operation would have to be followed by a ^PQ. Although it would satisfy the printer, you cannot use only the ^PQ command to terminate scripting. WordStar scripting commands, like all its toggles, must always be used in pairs or strange things can happen.

The USR functions are also useful for changing modes and type styles. Since there is little room on the Print Menu to indicate how these functions are assigned, it is a good idea to strive for whatever mnemonic qualities you can achieve. In our example, USR1, accessed by ^PQ, is used to switch to the ML92's correspondence mode, the Q standing for Quality. We now need a way to get back, so the codes for switching to what Okidata calls the data processing mode are entered at USR2. To make this switch you enter a ^PW at the appropriate place in your text file. (A usable mnemonic for the W in this case is Worse, putting it in terms of print quality.)

The entry at USR3 could best be termed a wild card. It is set up to send only an Escape code in response to a ^PE in text (E for Escape). The printer then responds to following text characters as if they were a control sequence, which in fact they are. When sufficient characters are read to complete what the printer recognizes as a command sequence, it executes the command and reverts to printing. This application is handy and versatile, but you have to remember what you're doing to avoid trouble. (This, by the way, is one time when you do not use hex. Use the ASCII equivalent in text; WordStar does the converting.) The last of this group, USR4, is assigned to select condensed type at 17 cpi using the ^PR command. (Mnemonically the R could stand for "Real small.") This font is useful for special purposes, but remember that it will result in rather narrow columns unless you extend the right margin and are prepared to do a lot of horizontal scrolling.

The next pair of entries at RIBBON and RIBOFF illustrate not only a useful application but an adaptation of functions to a purpose other than their original design purpose. (This is a useful technique which you can often use to advantage.) Since the ML92 does not have provisions for ribbon color changes, these functions are used to switch to and from the printer's double-width character mode. This mode is useful for emphasis, as in titles and headings, but should be used only on lines by itself because WordStar's column count is meaningless in this mode. It can also be used with other print enhancements such as bold or double strike.

The RIBBON/RIBOFF functions also operate like a toggle. At the first encounter of ^PY in a file, WordStar sends the sequence at RIBBON to the printer. At the second, it sends the sequence at RIBOFF. Therefore, the text string to be printed in double-width characters is enclosed by ^PY commands. In the example shown, the RIBOFF sequence returns the printer to 10 cpi, but by substituting the appropriate codes, you can easily make this 12 cpi if you normally use that pitch. As a finishing touch you could look up the Print Menu in WSMSGS.OVR and change the entry for Y to something more indicative of your actual usage.

Our final entries are for the print initiation and finishing strings, PSINIT and PSFINI. In the example, codes are entered to clear the print buffer, home the print head, and set the printer to data processing mode. Although these are typical applications for these functions, you can use them to preset a variety of printer modes or states and to clear them or set the printer to another state at the end of a printing job.

The enhancements described here make it unnecessary to use Okidata's Plug 'N Play module for the ML92/93. In fact, it is a disadvantage to do so, since you have to give up 12 cpi and are forced to use an unhandy command sequence for subscripts and superscripts.

DRIVING A HYBRID PRINTER

The Texas Instruments model 855 represents an emerging breed of matrix printer that capitalizes on the inherent flexibility of this printer type by incorporating features of both daisy-wheel and matrix printers. Although its characters are not quite up to the quality of daisy or thimble printers, it offers the advantages of fast draft or slower letter-quality modes, quick font changes, and extended graphics capabilities. Since it can operate in either a conventional non-microspacing mode (POSMTH = FF) or a microspacing mode (POSMTH = 01), we'll refer to this class as hybrid printers.

TI calls the 855's two basic operating modes Data Processing (DP) and Word Processing (WP). Although it is possible to meld features from both modes into a single operating mode, distinctions are such that you could end up with too much compromise. It is better to create two working versions of WordStar, one for DP mode and the other for WP mode. This also bypasses the problem of how to shift back and forth between appropriate values of POSMTH, which of course cannot be done by WordStar command. For brevity, details on implementation are less generalized than preceding discussions on the ML92 and microspacing printer considerations, and you may find it helpful to read these sections before proceeding.

To implement the DP mode, first run the Install program to establish a baseline. (Use any matrix printer except the default IBM parallel routine in version 3.3.) A set of recommended enhancements is shown in figure 9-4. As before, to avoid errors and to record your data, you should set up a worksheet as shown in figure 9-2. Using tables at the end of this chapter, then look up and enter function addresses for your version of WordStar.

Figure 9-4. Typical Enhanced Functions For A TI-855 (DP Mode)

Function	Lgth	Value(s)	Description	Access
PALT	03	12 1B 7A	Cancel compr, set 12 pitch	^PA
PSTD	03	12 1B 79	Cancel compr, set 10 pitch	^PN
ROLUP	02	1B 5E	Superscript On	^PT
ROLDOW	02	1B 76	Subscript On	^PV
USR1	02	1B 71	Select quality print mode	^PQ
USR2	02	1B 64	Select draft print mode	^PW
USR3	01	1B	Wild Card - see text	^PE
USR4	01	0F	Select compressed print	^PR
RIBBON	01	0E	Double-width characters	^PY
RIBOFF	01	14	Cancel double-width	^PY
PSINIT	05	1B 40 1B 64 0D	Selects DP mode, draft	——
PSFINI	05	1B 40 1B 64 0D	printing, CR	——

With the setup shown in figure 9-4, boldface or shadow printing and selection of font module sockets are accomplished by using the wild-card function (^PE), which of course can be used as well to invoke functions you have not otherwise provided for as explained in the preceding section. In text you use ^PEE to begin shadow printing and ^PEF to end. To select a font module, insert ^PEf plus the socket number—as in ^PEf2. Contrary to usual WordStar permissiveness, **be sure to observe upper and lower case** for the added characters when using the wild-card function, since the printer interprets them literally. Again, you might profitably change the Print Menu label for the ribbon change function to reflect its real usage.

To implement your word processing version of WordStar for the 855, begin by running Install for either a basic Diablo 630 or a Qume Sprint 11. (The Qume codes are a little closer, but the difference is slight.) The required modifications to D-labeled functions are shown in figure 9-5. As before, it will be necessary to look up the addresses for your version of WordStar, and use of a worksheet is again recommended.

Figure 9-5. Function Changes For TI-855 In WP Mode

Label	ASCII Code	Lgth	Hex Equiv	Function/Notes
DVMRNG		——	56	85 decimal + 1
DHRNG		——	FE (see text)	255 decimal + 1
DPHSPC	Esc Spc	02	1B 20	Print spl char #1
DPHRUB	Esc /	02	1B 2F	Print spl char #2
PSINIT	CR Esc CR P	04	0D 1B 0D 50	CR, initiate WP mode
PSFINI	CR Esc @	03	0D 1B 40	CR, reset to DP mode

The required changes are typical in all respects except one: the value of DHRNG is truncated slightly to meet WordStar format requirements, but the practical effect of this is only to abbreviate a range already broader than needed except in a most unusual situation. If you want a different printer initialization or finishing string, insert the appropriate sequence at PSINIT or PSFINI. Useful functions like draft printing (Esc d) and font module changes can be implemented with required entries at USR functions and RIBBON/RIBOFF. Be careful about implementing other features like bold or shadow printing, bidirectional printing, auto-justify, automatic underscore, pitch changes, and proportional spacing. In the WP mode these functions are all handled internally by WordStar, and attempts to implement duplicate commands, internally or externally, can cause conflicts and strange results.

PRINT FUNCTION ADDRESS LISTINGS

Table 9-1 lists addresses, labels, formats, and access commands, where applicable, for all printer control functions. Two addresses are given for each function, the first applying to version 3.3, the second applying to versions 3.24 and earlier. As previously noted, some fields require a length byte to indicate how many characters follow, even if the following entry is only a single byte. Fields requiring a length byte are indicated by 00 in the length column. Those which do not need a length byte have a double dash (——) in the length column. When entries are present in length and value columns they are default values and are modified by Install as required for supported printers. The bytes shown in the value column indicate the total number of bytes available for the associated function.

Remember that the length byte tells WordStar how many of the following command bytes to read. If it is zero, the command is in effect disabled even though there may be entries in the command field. Be sure the value in the length byte is consistent with the number of bytes you want read as the related command.

Before you implement these functions for your particular printer, be sure you understand their implications and constraints by reading preceding sections on functional descriptions and their practical application.

Table 9-1. Address Listings For Printer Control Functions

3.3 Addr	3.24 Addr	Label	Lgth	Value(s)	Function	Access
0746	0746	POSMTH	——	00	Specifies printer type	——
0747	0747	BLDSTR	——	02	Number of strikes for bold	^PB
0748	0748	DBLSTR	——	02	Number of strikes for dbl	^PD
0749	0749			00 00 00	Reserved bytes	
074C	074C	PSCRLF	02	0D 0A 00 00	Carriage Ret, Line Feed	——
				00 00 00 00	space for add'l entries	
				00 00		
0757	0757	PSCR	02	0D 00 00 00	Carriage Ret, null	——
075E	075E	PSHALF	00	00 00 00 00	For Carriage Ret, half LF	——
				00 00		
0765	0765	PBACKS	01	08 00 00 00	Printer backspace character	——
				00		
076B	076B	PALT	00	00 00 00 00	Select alternate pitch	^PA
0770	0770	PSTD	00	00 00 00 00	Return to standard pitch	^PN
0775	0775	ROLUP	00	00 00 00 00	Roll for superscript	^PT
077A	077A	ROLDOW	00	00 00 00 00	Roll for subscript	^PV
077F	077F	USR1	00	00 00 00 00	User selectable feature #1	^PQ
0784	0784	USR2	00	00 00 00 00	User selectable feature #2	^PW
0789	0789	USR3	00	00 00 00 00	User selectable feature #3	^PE
078E	078E	USR4	00	00 00 00 00	User selectable feature #4	^PR
0793	0793	RIBBON	00	00 00 00 00	Select alt ribbon color	^PY
0798	0798	RIBOFF	00	00 00 00 00	Reset ribbon color	^PY
079D	079D	PSINIT	01	0D 00 00 00	Printer initiation string	——
				00 00 00 00		
				00 00 00 00	space for add'l entries	
				00 00 00 00		
07AE	07AE	PSFINI	00	00 00 00 00	Printer finishing string	——
				00 00 00 00		
				00 00 00 00	space for add'l entries	
				00 00 00 00		
07BF	07BF	00 00			Reserved bytes	
07C1	07C1	SOCHR	——	2D	Strike-out character (–)	^PX
07C2	07C2	ULCHR	——	5F	Underline character (_)	^PS
07C3	07C3	PRINIT		00 00 00	Not used for IBM PC	
07C6	07C6	PRFINI		00 00 00	Not used for IBM PC	
07C9	07C9	CSWTCH	——	00	Selects printer driver	——
07CA	07CA	HAVBSY	——	FF	Should be 00 for IBM PC	
0879	0879	PROTCL	——	00	Protocol, serial only	——
087A	087A	EAKBSZ	——	00	Applies only if PROTCL = 1	——
087B					Not used	
087C	087C	DVMILE	02	1B 1E 00 00	VMI Lead-in; Diablo, Qume	——

Table 9-1. Address Listings For Printer Control Functions (Continued)

3.3 Addr	3.24 Addr	Label	Lgth	Value(s)	Function	Access
0881	none	DVMITR	02	1B 02	VMI Trailer; NEC 3550 (v3.3)	——
0886	0881	DVMMIN	——	01 00	VMI Minimum; Diablo, Qume	——
0888	0883	DVMRNG	——	7E 00	VMI Range +1; Diablo, Qume	——
088A	0885	DHMILE	02	1B 1F 00 00	HMI Lead-in; Diablo, Qume	——
088F	088A	DHMIFG	——	00	HMI Flag; set FF for 60ths	——
0890	088B	DHMIN	——	01 00	HMI Minimum; Diablo, Qume	——
0892	088D	DHRNG	——	7E 00	HMI Range +1; Diablo, Qume	——
0894	088F	DFWD	02	1B 35 00 00	Print forward; Diablo, Qume	——
0899	0894	DBAK	02	1B 36 00 00	Print backwd; Diablo, Qume	——
089E	0899	DSP	01	20 00 00 00	Daisy space	——
08A3	089E	DBS	01	08 00 00 00	Daisy backspace	——
08A8	08A3	DLF	01	0A 00 00 00	Daisy line feed	——
08AD	08A8	DRLF	02	1B 0A 00 00	Daisy reverse line feed	——
08B2	08AD	DPHSPC	02	1B 59 00	Print spl char; Diablo	^PF
08B6	08B1	DPHRUB	02	1B 5A 00	Print alt spl char; Diablo	^PG

NOTES:

1) Addresses in first column apply to version 3.3.
2) Addresses in second column apply to versions 3.24 and earlier.
3) Double dash indicates no value required or does not apply.
4) Locations 07CB through 0878 are omitted. (Contains code for printer drivers, which normally do not need to be modified and are not easily patchable.)

10
PROPORTIONAL SPACING WITH WORDSTAR

Many users have wished aloud that WordStar supported proportional spacing; it seems few are aware that the program already does this on many daisy-wheel printers. Perhaps more surprising, WordStar can print proportionally with not only an unpublicized special command but with standard printing commands as well. One reason for the mystery is that this feature is not officially supported or documented in WordStar manuals. Another is that table errors in the program for some time have obscured just how good WordStar printing can be. With moderate effort the proportional spacing feature can be made to work well except for minor quirks and will produce printed output approaching typesetting quality. Special print wheels are not mandatory; many standard wheels can also give excellent results.

Buried within WS.COM is a proportional spacing table containing 96 entries for the basic ASCII character set or its variations found on typical daisy print wheels. The two-digit entries for each character are relative width values. These numeric entries control horizontal carriage movement for each character on microspacing printers such as the NEC Spinwriters, Diablo, Qume, Silver-Reed, and other models.

A table error exists in both 3.24 and 3.3, but in slightly different form. In both, however, it causes improper spacings for several characters, being too wide in some cases and too narrow in others. It can be corrected with relatively simple patches to be shown later; the result is significant improvement in the appearance of printed output obtained with the standard printing commands. With a few added steps you can also optimize the table for your particular setup. This results in further enhancement of output appearance, both in regular printing and when using the undocumented ^PP proportional spacing command.

More widely known among WordStar's documented features is one which MicroPro terms microjustification. This is a more sophisticated form of justification involving the use of micro-spaces distributed throughout a line of print. But before we get into mechanics of program modifications, it is useful to review principles on which justification and proportional spacing are based. As you will see, the two are closely related.

A FEW BASICS

In printing the term justified means that lines in a text column are adjusted to be the same length. Thus, you get text columns with straight edges on both right and left. This is considered by many people to be more professional looking because of its similarity to commercial typesetting. The simplest form of justification is done by adding spaces between words to spread out each line of print so that all are the same length (excepting, of course, indentations and lines at ends of paragraphs.) With narrow columns and long words, however, this basic process can result in relatively large amounts of white space between words—not a desirable appearance.

To overcome this problem, WordStar follows quality typesetting practice by adding small amounts of white space between characters within a word to reduce excessive interword spacing. This is done in very small increments (normally 1/120-inch each) to avoid creating new appearance problems by solving the original; hence the term microjustification.

We now have a basis for true proportional spacing, which by definition means that horizontal movement of carriage or printhead is proportional to the width of a printed character. Thus, the movement for narrow letters like i or l is less than that for wide letters such as m or w. The value for each character is commonly stored in a width table. In principle the mechanism used for microspaced justification is the same as that needed for proportional spacing. However, it's not this simple in practice.

In the typesetting world there are literally hundreds of different type styles. While they share general relationships regarding relative widths of characters, there is wide variety in the details. The situation is similar with typewriters and their descendents, daisy-wheel printers. There aren't as many different type styles to cope with, but there still are numerous variations in character width ratios. There is high likelihood, therefore, that a width table which is correct for one type font, or in our case a specific daisy wheel or thimble, will be less than optimum for another.

Using a modern, intelligent printer can further complicate matters. Many of these printers can be set up for proportional spacing. They have proportional print wheels and may have internal width tables and related logic. A ready-made situation for conflict exists when the word processing program attempts to control character widths to justify printed lines at the same time the printer is trying to space characters proportionally.

At the very least, justification combined with proportional spacing involves considerable amounts of computation. First, the program must examine complete lines of text, since each printed line must be the same length. It must determine what characters are present in a line and look up the relative widths for each. Then it must count the interword spaces and determine if justification producing acceptable appearance can be done by adjusting these spaces only. If not, it must do the calculations necessary to insert microspaces between characters. For optimum appearance in the printed line, these spaces must be in proportion to the relative width of each character. This involves even more computing. Not only do necessary algorithms become complex, the processing can be time consuming. As a result, programs which support proportional spacing at all may incorporate only a simplified version or one that works well under some conditions but not so well under others.

All this may sound discouraging, but its real purpose is to provide insight and to prepare you to make some necessary compromises. You will find that factors such as column widths and average length of words in a column have a direct bearing on whether to use proportional spacing with simple justification involving interword spacing only, microjustification, or no justification (ragged right). Perhaps to avoid a need for tinkering, WordStar in stock form makes most of the required trade-offs for you, but the program contains the means for you to do considerable optimizing.

HOW PROPORTIONAL SPACING WORKS IN WORDSTAR

If you are using a microspacing printer, which includes most daisy-wheel printers as well as some newer matrix models, the proportional spacing table is used for both ragged-right and justified text. It is necessary, however, to have formed paragraphs for proportional spacing to occur. This happens automatically when word-wrap is on and a line is long enough for word-wrap to occur. It does not occur for the last line in a paragraph or for stand-alone lines (i.e., set off by carriage returns). For proportional spacing to occur in these lines, Paragraph Reform (^B) must be used, even though there is no visible on-screen effect.

The reason for this is that relative width values in the proportional spacing table are invoked whenever the high-order bits marking the ends of words are set, as occurs in word-wrap and reforming operations. The second condition is that the Printer Overstrike Method (POSMTH) must be set to 01, indicating a microspacing printer. Normally this value is automatically set when you run the Install program for such a printer.

The table contains two-digit entries for each of the ASCII characters covered. The left digit controls relative width (the amount the carriage or printhead moves for a given character) for regular printing under the above conditions. The right digit controls relative width when the undocumented proportional spacing command ^PP is in effect. (This command is embedded in text and is a toggle; you invoke it once to start and again to stop.) In its practical effect, therefore, the table acts like two tables, each part containing a unique set of character width values invoked under different command conditions. This creates interesting possibilities in setting up the table for two different print wheels.

It is not necessary to use a special proportional-spacing type wheel to print with proportional spacing in WordStar. In fact it is easier to set up the table for a regular non-proportional wheel. Designers of type fonts for daisy-wheel typewriters or printers having fixed escapements usually design characters in a few groups, each having as much as possible the same width while maintaining good appearance. Fonts designed for proportional spacing are not subject to this constraint, and widths of individual characters can be whatever the designer considers pleasing. Variations in relative widths, and the esperimenting you may have to do to obtain proper table entries, will probably be less in most cases for standard type wheels. Depending on the selection of wheels available for your printer, you may still opt for a proportional wheel. While this may involve additional effort and expense, it is still mostly a matter of personal choice.

CORRECTING EXISTING TABLE ERRORS

It is best to begin by checking to see if the table error is present in your copy and correcting it if necessary. Even if you do not wish then to optimize the proportional spacing capability, this correction is worth the modest effort it requires. If you are using a microspacing printer, an improvement in print quality will be immediately evident.

The most obvious clues are too narrow spacings for lower case letters m and w, and too wide spacing for lower case l's. Other spacing errors are present as well, but these are the easiest to spot. A conclusive test is to examine WS.COM location 0910 in version 3.24 or 0915 in 3.3 using the dump (D) command in Debug. If the value is hex 66 in either one, you have the problem. In both versions an entry near the middle of the table was left out. This caused all following entries to move up, skewing the character width values. For the fixes below, enter only the data shown in bold.

The following applies to version 3.24 only:

A>**debug ws.com <Ret>**
-m 08f6 0922 08f7 <Ret>
-e 08f6 <Ret>
22BD:08f6 54.**56 <Ret>**
-w <Ret>
Writing XXXX bytes
-q <Ret>
A>

The following applies to version 3.3 only:

A>**debug ws.com <Ret>**
-m 08fa 0927 08fb <Ret>
-w <Ret>
Writing XXXX bytes
-q <Ret>
A>

The preceding patches use the Move (M) command in Debug to bump the width table entries back down a notch, beginning where the error originally occurred. In 3.24 it is also necessary to correct the value for the entry following that point; this is not necessary in 3.3.

Figure 10-1 shows how the patch and its result appear on the screen when applied to version 3.3. First we load Debug and WS.COM; then we dump the portion of memory containing the proportional spacing table, beginning at location 08C0. This is to illustrate the process; it is not necessary for the actual patch. Note that the table actually begins at location 08C9 and ends at 0927. This is one location short of where it should end (the table entry for the letter Q was left out). After making the patch we again dump the same area of memory. The table now ends at 0928 as it should.

These fixes get the table back to a baseline which, although improved, still may not be optimum for your printer and print wheel. Left-hand digits of the table were set up originally for an early Diablo printer using a print wheel of undetermined specifications. The right-hand digits are for a Qume Theme print wheel. If you wish to make further improvements, changes to the width values for individual characters will be necessary.

HOW TO OPTIMIZE PROPORTIONAL SPACING

Obtaining optimum print appearance requires choosing a print wheel or thimble whose actual character widths are compatible with WordStar printing parameters, setting width values in the spacing table which are correct for the wheel or thimble you intend to use, and selecting an appropriate pitch with WordStar printing commands. This generally involves tighter character spacings than occur with the usual printer setup, especially at 10 cpi.

Before we get into the optimizing process itself, let's take another look at what you will be working with. Referring again to figure 10-1, note that each address in the spacing table contains two digits. Each pair of digits is a set of width values for a specific printed character. The left digit is used in standard printing; the right digit is used only when the special proportional printing command (^PP) is used. These width values are used by WordStar to tell the printer how far to move the carriage for each character. Note also the ASCII part of the dump, shown at far right; your debugger translates hex values at each location as if they were characters. In fact, they are not. Debug doesn't know or care that it is the numeric values themselves which matter in this instance, but WordStar program logic does. WordStar associates a given character with its width value by the position of the width value in the table.

In effect, the spacing table is in two parts, since the left and right digits of each pair operate under different command conditions. Although not strictly accurate, for convenience we will refer to these parts as the left and right sides. For standard print commands (^PP not used) we must optimize the left-hand digits for the particular wheel to be used.

You will note that the digits range in value from 2 to 7. The latter is the highest value that can be used because of the way WordStar program logic operates internally. Each increment in width value is 1/60 of an inch (approximately .017). Therefore, the maximum available width is 7/60 or about .117 of an inch. However, this must include an allowance for white space between adjacent characters.

If maximum physical widths of individual characters are not excessive, a 10-pitch wheel such as Courier-10 can produce very good results if other parameters are properly set up. In general, printed character widths should not exceed about .090 inches. Usually the widest are M's and W's in both upper and lower case. The most accurate way of measuring widths is with a calibrated optical comparator—often used in graphic arts and printing but hardly average household or even general business equipment. A practical substitute is to print a page of text using your 10-pitch wheel at 12 cpi (^PA) with justification (^OJ) off. Do not use the ^PP or .CW commands. If most of the characters do not touch, and the overlap on those that do is slight, chances are the wheel will work with appropriate adjustments to the spacing table.

As good a way as any of optimizing the left-hand side of the table is through trial and error. Examine a page of text printed as described above, and look for combinations of characters where spacings appear too narrow or too wide. To avoid being misled by a particular combination, make up and print strings of dummy words of six or eight characters each, repeating next to each other those characters you suspect of improper table width values. Do this for both upper and lower case as well as special characters.

By this time you should have a fairly good idea of what direction to go in modifying specific values in the width table. The tables at the end of this chapter provide width-value addresses, each one related to a specific character. Using the Enter (E) command in Debug, display and modify the contents of a location as required. After doing this, repeat the preceding tests to verify results. It is best to change a given value one increment at a time (i.e., a 5 to a 6 or vice versa, etc.), and you may find that more than one iteration is required. To avoid later inter-word spacing problems within printed lines, make these values no larger than necessary to maintain separation between characters.

If you plan to use a pitch setting of 12, a good choice as will be explained shortly, width settings should not exceed an average value of 5. The reason is this: at a pitch of 12 cpi the average space available per character is 1/12 or .083 inch, including inter-character white space. Since width table increments are in 60ths, a width setting of 5 is equal to 5/60 or also .083 inch. Unfortunately, you cannot simply average all width values in the table to determine the average character width, because in typical text characters appear with different frequencies. As a practical matter this rule of thumb applies mostly to lower-case letters.

Since the left-hand set of digits acts independently of the right, it is possible to set up the table for two different type wheels requiring different character widths. An example is shown in table 10-2. The left values are for Courier 10 to be used with a pitch setting of 12 (^PA). This produces what is known in typesetting circles as a desirable "tight" set. The right-hand values are for Letter Gothic on a 12-pitch wheel. Table 10-3 is set up for a Letter Gothic wheel on both sides. It was devised mainly to determine what differences in printed output appearance might result between the two halves of the table. There are almost none, but because of differences in program logic, required width values differ slightly. Table 10-4 is the same as 10-2 except for version 3.24 addresses.

All these examples are for print wheels used on a Silver-Reed model EXP-550 printer. Some experimenting probably will be necessary to arrive at optimum values for your particular combination of printer and print wheel or type font. The examples shown may be useful as a starting point.

If you wish to use a special proportional-spacing print wheel, enter appropriate width values on the right-hand side of the table. Usually these values are specified in your printer manual, but even these may benefit from some fine tuning. If specified width values exceed 7 (based on 1/60-inch increments) you will have to scale them down to fit. Given the wide variety of wheels and thimbles available, it is possible that some may not work well at all. Some may have character arrangements grossly incompatible with your keyboard and the character display on your monitor, and many do not have full ASCII character sets. But if you come across a proportional type style that you simply cannot do without, try it. However, its character sequence must be compatible with WordStar's or you will get printed gibberish.

The final step is to select pitch settings that are appropriate for the other parameters you have established through your choices of print wheels and width values in the spacing table. As you may have surmised by now, these three functions—print wheel characteristics, width values, and pitch settings—are like the three legs of a triangle. A change of one influences the others.

The easiest approach results when you have a 10-pitch standard wheel or equivalent proportional wheel (with relatively large characters) which can be used at a pitch setting of 12 with appropriate width values in the table. Column widths and margins fall neatly into place without mental gymnastics. Remember, however, that this can be overdone. You are then printing twelve characters in a space loosely designed for ten, relying on the fact that average character widths are well under maximum widths. Most of the time this causes no problems and produces fine quality. If you print narrow columns, on the other hand, combinations of long words and wide letters can cause inadequate interword spacings. This happens because paragraph forming operations "borrow" space from between words to get the space needed to add between characters. The effect is especially noticeable in stand-alone lines and in those at the ends of paragraphs. Conversely, high percentages of narrow letters in lines can result in excessive spacings.

If you wish to use a wheel with relatively narrow letters, such as most 12-pitch type styles and many proportional wheels, it may be necessary to use .CW dot commands to achieve character spacings tight enough for optimum readability and appearance. In some cases settings as low as .CW8, equal to 15 cpi, may be required. To a degree this is at odds with our overall objectives, one of which is to make WordStar easier to use. Column widths and margin settings are no longer as direct or as simple to manage, and in-text ruler lines may be required to keep things sorted out. These are not large obstacles, but they do add baggage to word processing operations.

WHAT TO DO IF YOU ENCOUNTER PROBLEMS

If you are using a so-called intelligent printer, especially one with built-in proportional spacing capability, you may find that getting it to print proportionally defies your best efforts. First, check to be sure that the printer is properly installed for WordStar (see the printer chapter), especially that POSMTH is set to 01, that the other parameters for a microspacing printer are correctly set, and that all switches in the printer itself are also set properly. If the condition persists even after you have double-checked to be sure you have followed correct procedure and no errors are present, the problem may be that proportional spacing routines in the printer are conflicting with those of WordStar.

In such a case it will be necessary to disable this mechanism in the printer. With some printers this is readily done by resetting a switch inside. Others may require special escape codes, which should be detailed in the printer instruction manual. For this situation it may be necessary to use one of the WordStar USR patch areas (also described in the printer chapter) to enable sending the required codes. Finally, some printers may require an internal modification. Should this be true it is best to consult the manufacturer or to look for another printer.

The problem might also be remedied by nothing more complex than turning off the printer's internal bidirectional printing switch if the unit is so equipped. WordStar sends the necessary codes to the printer automatically as part of its printing routines.

PROPORTIONAL SPACING HINTS AND VARIATIONS

When using the preceding schemes, keep certain guidelines in mind. Try to avoid narrow column widths if long words and strings of capital letters are involved. Using justification in some applications alleviates too-tight spacings because of the spaces added between characters. At other times it can result in either too much or too little interword spacing. Ragged-right (^OJ off) margins also have their place. In short, it is necessary to fit techniques to applications, as is true even without the modifications.

In general, do not use Paragraph Reform (^B) on capitalized headings. The borrowing of interword space that then occurs to obtain adequate inter-character spacing can result in improper overall distribution of space and unsatisfactory appearance. It is usually best to switch back to 10-pitch (^PN) for headings, especially if they are in bold. A side benefit is that they will also appear visually larger and bolder as a result of the added spacing. This technique will require a subsequent positioning adjustment if you want centered headings and text below is in 12-pitch. If you are using a text width of 76 columns at 12-pitch, deleting four spaces to the left of the heading after you center it (^OC) will maintain approximate centering.

As mentioned earlier, you should use Paragraph Reform in text to assure that proportional spacing will occur in lines which have not been formed by normal word-wrap operations. When you revise a paragraph and add words, it is always a good idea to follow up with a ^B.

There are two flags in WS.COM which are also relevant to proportional spacing on microspacing printers. The first is labeled DNPROS. It is of limited utility since what it does when set is to turn all proportional spacing off. It may be useful in the early stages to check the effects of various pitch settings on a specific print wheel prior to selecting width values for the spacing table. Normally it is set to zero; if you wish to turn proportional spacing off, patch it to FF. If you use this function, be sure to patch it back to zero when finished. Otherwise, you may wonder later why proportional spacing refuses to work.

The second flag, labeled DMJWB, is more useful. When set, it modifies the justification algorithm so that less space is added between characters to justify a line. Thus, more space remains between words. Depending on page format, this may produce more readable and attractive printed output. Normally the flag is set to zero; patch to FF to turn this feature on.

In conclusion, remember how width values in the spacing table are used. The left side is normally used and requires no special commands to invoke. The right side is used only with the ^PP command. Finally, you may find a combination of standard print wheel and width values that produces excellent results and elect to stop there. If you opt for the extra work involved with a proportional wheel, you may do even better.

Figure 10-1. WS 3.3 Proportional Spacing Table, Before And After Fix

```
A>debug ws.com
-d08c0
04D7:08C0  00 00 00 00 00 00 00 00-00 52 43 44 54 54 56 56   .........RCDTTVV
04D7:08D0  32 43 43 54 54 42 54 32-53 54 54 54 54 54 54 54   2CCTTBT2STTTTTTT
04D7:08E0  54 54 54 43 42 54 54 54-54 56 55 55 55 56 55 55   TTTCBTTTTVUUUVUU
04D7:08F0  56 56 53 53 56 55 66 56-56-54 56 54 55 56 56 67   VVSSVUfVVTVTUVVg
04D7:0900  56 56 55 54 56 54 56 55-54 54 54 54 54 54 53 54   VVUTVTVUTTTTTTST
04D7:0910  54 52 52 54 52 66 54 54-54 54 53 53 53 54 54 66   TRRTRfTTTTSSSTTf
04D7:0920  54 54 54 54 56 54 56 55-00 00 00 00 20 20 20 20   TTTTVTVU....
04D7:0930  20 20 20 20 20 20 20 00-00 00 00 00 00 00 00 00           .........
-m 08fa 0927 08fb
-w
Writing 5380 bytes
-d08c0
04D7:08C0  00 00 00 00 00 00 00 00-00 52 43 44 54 54 56 56   .........RCDTTVV
04D7:08D0  32 43 43 54 54 42 54 32-53 54 54 54 54 54 54 54   2CCTTBT2STTTTTTT
04D7:08E0  54 54 54 43 42 54 54 54-54 56 55 55 55 56 55 55   TTTCBTTTTVUUUVUU
04D7:08F0  56 56 53 53 56 55 66 56-56 54 56 56 54 55 56 56   VVSSVUfVVTVVTUVV
04D7:0900  67 56 56 55 54 56 54 56-55 54 54 54 54 54 54 53   gVVUTVTVUTTTTTTS
04D7:0910  54 54 52 52 54 52 66 54-54 54 54 53 53 53 54 54   TTRRTRfTTTTSSSTT
04D7:0920  66 54 54 54 54 56 54 56-55 00 00 00 20 20 20 20   fTTTTVTVU...
04D7:0930  20 20 20 20 20 20 20 00-00 00 00 00 00 00 00 00           .........
-q

A>
```

Table 10-1. Proportional Printing Flag Locations

Label	3.24 Loc	3.3 Loc	Std Val	Notes
DNPROS	08BF	O8C4	00	Patch FF to set
DMJWB	08C0	O8C5	00	Patch FF to set

Table 10-2. WordStar Proportional Spacing Values

Addr	*Std*	*Mod*	*Char*	*Addr*	*Std*	*Mod*	*Char*
08C9	52	53	ph spc	08F9	53	64	P
08CA	43	44	!	08FA	56	64	Q
08CB	44	43	"	08FB	56	64	R
08CC	54	54	#	08FC	54	64	S
08CD	54	54	$	08FD	55	64	T
08CE	56	54	%	08FE	56	64	U
08CF	56	54	&	08FF	56	64	V
08D0	32	33	'	0900	67	65	W
08D1	43	43	(	0901	56	63	X
08D2	43	43	)	0902	56	63	Y
08D3	54	54	*	0903	55	63	Z
08D4	54	54	+	0904	54	44	[
08D5	42	43	,	0905	56	54	\
08D6	54	54	–	0906	54	44	]
08D7	32	43	.	0907	56	54	^
08D8	53	54	/	0908	55	55	_
08D9	54	54	0	0909	54	54	`
08DA	54	54	1	090A	54	54	a
08DB	54	54	2	090B	54	54	b
08DC	54	54	3	090C	54	54	c
08DD	54	54	4	090D	54	54	d
08DE	54	54	5	090E	54	54	e
08DF	54	54	6	090F	53	54	f
08E0	54	54	7	0910	54	54	g
08E1	54	54	8	0911	54	54	h
08E2	54	54	9	0912	53	53	i
08E3	43	43	:	0913	52	53	j
08E4	42	43	;	0914	54	54	k
08E5	54	54	<	0915	52	43	l
08E6	54	54	=	0916	66	65	m
08E7	54	54	>	0917	54	54	n
08E8	54	55	?	0918	54	54	o
08E9	56	55	@	0919	54	54	p
08EA	55	64	A	091A	54	54	q
08EB	55	64	B	091B	53	54	r
08EC	55	64	C	091C	53	54	s
08ED	56	64	D	091D	53	54	t
08EE	55	64	E	091E	54	54	u
08EF	55	64	F	091F	54	54	v
08F0	56	64	G	0920	66	65	w
08F1	56	64	H	0921	54	54	x
08F2	53	53	I	0922	54	54	y
08F3	53	64	J	0923	54	54	z
08F4	56	64	K	0924	54	54	{
08F5	55	64	L	0925	56	54	|
08F6	66	65	M	0926	54	54	}
08F7	56	64	N	0927	56	54	~
08F8	56	64	O	0928	55	55	ph rub

Note: WS 3.3, PC-DOS - Optimized for Courier-10 (left) and Letter Gothic.

Table 10-3. WordStar Proportional Spacing Values

Addr	*Std*	*Mod*	*Char*	*Addr*	*Std*	*Mod*	*Char*
08C9	52	53	ph spc	08F9	53	54	P
08CA	43	44	!	08FA	56	54	Q
08CB	44	43	"	08FB	56	54	R
08CC	54	54	#	08FC	54	54	S
08CD	54	54	$	08FD	55	54	T
08CE	56	54	%	08FE	56	54	U
08CF	56	54	&	08FF	56	54	V
08D0	32	33	'	0900	67	65	W
08D1	43	43	(	0901	56	54	X
08D2	43	43	)	0902	56	54	Y
08D3	54	54	*	0903	55	54	Z
08D4	54	54	+	0904	54	44	[
08D5	42	43	,	0905	56	54	\
08D6	54	54	–	0906	54	44	]
08D7	32	43	.	0907	56	54	^
08D8	53	54	/	0908	55	55	_
08D9	54	54	0	0909	54	54	`
08DA	54	54	1	090A	54	54	a
08DB	54	54	2	090B	54	54	b
08DC	54	54	3	090C	54	54	c
08DD	54	54	4	090D	54	54	d
08DE	54	54	5	090E	54	54	e
08DF	54	54	6	090F	53	54	f
08E0	54	54	7	0910	54	54	g
08E1	54	54	8	0911	54	54	h
08E2	54	54	9	0912	53	43	i
08E3	43	43	:	0913	52	53	j
08E4	42	43	;	0914	54	54	k
08E5	54	54	<	0915	52	43	l
08E6	54	54	=	0916	66	65	m
08E7	54	54	>	0917	54	54	n
08E8	54	55	?	0918	54	54	o
08E9	56	55	@	0919	54	54	p
08EA	55	64	A	091A	54	54	q
08EB	55	54	B	091B	53	54	r
08EC	55	54	C	091C	53	54	s
08ED	56	54	D	091D	53	54	t
08EE	55	54	E	091E	54	54	u
08EF	55	54	F	091F	54	54	v
08F0	56	54	G	0920	66	65	w
08F1	56	54	H	0921	54	54	x
08F2	53	43	I	0922	54	54	y
08F3	53	54	J	0923	54	54	z
08F4	56	54	K	0924	54	54	{
08F5	55	54	L	0925	56	54	|
08F6	66	65	M	0926	54	54	}
08F7	56	54	N	0927	56	54	~
08F8	56	54	O	0928	55	55	ph rub

Note: WS 3.3, PC-DOS. Optimized for Letter Gothic both sides

Table 10-4. WordStar Proportional Spacing Values

Addr	*Std*	*Mod*	*Char*	*Addr*	*Std*	*Mod*	*Char*
08C4	52	53	ph spc	08F4	53	64	P
08C5	43	44	!	08F5	56	64	Q
08C6	44	43	"	08F6	56	64	R
08C7	54	54	#	08F7	54	64	S
08C8	54	54	$	08F8	55	64	T
08C9	56	54	%	08F9	56	64	U
08CA	56	54	&	08FA	56	64	V
08CB	32	33	'	08FB	67	65	W
08CC	43	43	(	08FC	56	63	X
08CD	43	43	)	08FD	56	63	Y
08CE	54	54	*	08FE	55	63	Z
08CF	54	54	+	08FF	54	44	[
08D0	42	43	,	0900	56	54	\
08D1	54	54	–	0901	54	44	]
08D2	32	43	.	0902	56	54	^
08D3	53	54	/	0903	55	55	_
08D4	54	54	0	0904	54	54	`
08D5	54	54	1	0905	54	54	a
08D6	54	54	2	0906	54	54	b
08D7	54	54	3	0907	54	54	c
08D8	54	54	4	0908	54	54	d
08D9	54	54	5	0909	54	54	e
08DA	54	54	6	090A	53	54	f
08DB	54	54	7	090B	54	54	g
08DC	54	54	8	090C	54	54	h
08DD	54	54	9	090D	53	53	i
08DE	43	43	:	090E	52	53	j
08DF	42	43	;	090F	54	54	k
08E0	54	54	<	0910	52	43	l
08E1	54	54	=	0911	66	65	m
08E2	54	54	>	0912	54	54	n
08E3	54	55	?	0913	54	54	o
08E4	56	55	@	0914	54	54	p
08E5	55	64	A	0915	54	54	q
08E6	55	64	B	0916	53	54	r
08E7	55	64	C	0917	53	54	s
08E8	56	64	D	0918	53	54	t
08E9	55	64	E	0919	54	54	u
08EA	55	64	F	091A	54	54	v
08EB	56	64	G	091B	66	65	w
08EC	56	64	H	091C	54	54	x
08ED	53	53	I	091D	54	54	y
08EE	53	64	J	091E	54	54	z
08EF	56	64	K	091F	54	54	{
08F0	55	64	L	0920	56	54	|
08F1	66	65	M	0921	54	54	}
08F2	56	64	N	0922	56	54	~
08F3	56	64	O	0923	55	55	ph rub

Note: addresses are for WS.COM V3.24, PC-DOS

11
OTHER USEFUL MODIFICATIONS AND DATA

In a subject as broad as WordStar customizing there are bound to be a few topics that don't fit comfortably within some larger discussion. This does not necessarily mean they are less important but mainly that they are either complete by themselves or are of specialized interest. This is the case with topics presented here.

Among these are modifications to the USER-1 area mentioned in Chapter 2 but bypassed then, including how to set timing parameters for the cursor and messages, changing the default disk drive, setting the horizontal scrolling distance, and how to eliminate the version 3.3 function key display—which covers general use of the twenty-fifth screen line as well. Also included are details on setting up the automatic backspace table and a discussion of WordStar's usage of high-order bits.

Addresses listed at the end of this chapter apply to all PC versions of WordStar unless otherwise noted.

SETTING DISPLAY TIMING PARAMETERS

Beginning at location 02CF in WS.COM are five consecutive bytes that set timing parameters, labeled DEL1 through DEL5. The first two are for cursor on-off cycles, and the next three are for delay times associated with various messages, display of menus following entry of a command prefix, and rewrites of text to the screen. Values can range from 1 (minimum delay) to 127 (7Fh). Addresses and normal values are shown in table 11-1.

Normally there is little reason to alter cursor timing factors, since they work well with normal values. DEL1 controls the "on" portion of the cycle, and DEL2 controls the "off" portion. If you wish to experiment with other values, MicroPro suggests that existing ratios be maintained.

Adjusting the value of DEL3 can be often useful. The most significant parameter it controls is the delay from the time you press a command prefix (^K, etc.) until the associated menu is displayed—that is unless you have suppressed menus with a help setting of 0 or 1. Here you can go in either direction. If you are using a combination of ProKey and regular commands, you may want the menu to show up immediately for help with regular commands that you don't use often. Reducing the value to 1 or 2 is then appropriate. You'll never see the menu for ProKey commands, because the second character is dispatched before time-out occurs, even at a low setting. On the other hand, if you are a slow typist but usually don't need the menus for regular commands, increasing the delay will give you more time to type the second character and prevent the menus from scrolling down. By experimenting you can arrive at the best compromise setting.

Altering values of DEL4 and DEL5 is also helpful. DEL4 controls the time that the verbose start-up routine referred to as a "sign-on" is held on screen, as well as the "new file" and "abandon edit" messages. These add little to program operation except real delays. DEL5 controls the delay for screen rewrite after horizontal scrolling. Try values as low as 1 or 2 for both to speed things up.

CHANGING THE DEFAULT DISK DRIVE

If you use more than two floppy disk drives, a hard disk, or a RAM disk, you may want to change the default drive. Not to be confused with the logged-on drive, which is where WordStar assumes your text files will be located, the default drive is where WordStar looks for program and overlay files. In version 3.3 the default drive can be changed from the Install program. Again, unless you are doing this as part of initial installation, Debug is considerably faster. In earlier versions the change must be made with Debug.

The default drive assignment is a simple, one-byte entry at location 02DC in WS.COM, using numeric values of 1 through 4 corresponding to drive letters A through D. The normal setting is 1 for drive A. This is all you need to change in 3.3, but earlier versions also require a short patch in WS.COM to enable the change. The patch is as follows with required entries shown in bold:

```
A>debug ws.com <Ret>
-e 1e04 <Ret>
XXXX:1E04 B1.90   01.90 <Ret>
-w <Ret>
Writing XXXX bytes
-q <Ret>
A>
```

If you make such a change, remember that program files you leave on another drive can be called from WordStar only if you include the drive letter designation with the call. An example is where you have set up a RAM disk as drive C and transfer only the main WordStar programs to it to save space. Any other programs you leave on drive A must be called with the A: prefix; otherwise, you will get a file-not-found error message.

MODIFYING THE HORIZONTAL SCROLLING DISTANCE

Often when you are editing, word smithing, and rearranging paragraphs, the sentence you're working on may extend beyond column 80, calling for a ^QD command to view the extended portion. The "window" then shifts right to let you see what's out there. But as you have no doubt noted, the ends of normal-length lines remain visible at left. This overlap is the horizontal scrolling distance, and it is normally set to 20 characters.

In many situations it would be helpful in a contextual sense to be able to see more of the main text. You can do this by increasing the hex entry for horizontal scrolling distance at WS.COM location 02DD. Doubling the normal value of 14h to 28h will increase the overlap to about half a normal line length, reducing the extended area displayed to approximately the same amount. This is obviously a compromise, so you may want to experiment with other values.

ELIMINATING THE ON-SCREEN FUNCTION KEY DISPLAY IN 3.3

Nestled among the many useful enhancements to version 3.3 is one which only the most restrained critics and reviewers have failed to assail. This is the display of function key assignments across the bottom of the screen. Not arranged like the function keys physically, it also uses a valuable line of space. What's worse, it is a distracting element in a screen area where we work most often. Fortunately, it's easy to get rid of.

A simple two-part patch excises it. The first part suppresses the display, and the second releases the twenty-fifth line for normal text use. Make entries shown below in bold. (Note: Although most earlier versions are already set up to use the full 25 screen lines, you may find one that does not. The part of this patch applying to location 0248 will correct it.)

```
A>debug ws.com <Ret>
-e 5041 <Ret>
XXXX:5041 8D.c3 <Ret>
-e 0248 <Ret>
XXXX:0248 18.19 <Ret>
-w <Ret>
Writing XXXX bytes
-q <Ret>
A>
```

If you feel the need for a guide to function key assignments, as indeed you probably will at first, it is easy to produce a handy reference card as described and illustrated in Chapter 8.

SETTING UP THE AUTOMATIC BACKSPACE TABLE

Useful primarily to those who write in a language other than English, an undocumented automatic backspace table is included in WS.COM. It is empty as the program is delivered but contains space for up to 10 entries of one byte each, normally accent marks. Whenever a character present in the table is typed in text, a ^PH command to overprint the next character is generated automatically. This feature therefore operates in reverse of the order you would instinctively use: you first type the accent mark and then the character to be accented. Actually, calling the table a backspace table is something of a misnomer, since most microspacing printers will print the two characters sequentially with no intervening carriage movement.

External factors limit the feature's utility, probably accounting for the fact that it is not touted. The PC keyboard has few accent marks, and standard printer character sets make the problem no easier. A further complication is that characters you put in this table will then be unhandy to use in stand-alone applications, although a solution to this problem is to create a custom version of the program dedicated to foreign language use. If you have a printer with a suitable print wheel or character set and are willing to put up with the lack of keyboard markings, this feature can be a time and keystroke saver, especially with heavily accented languages.

The table begins at location 0422 and is terminated by a zero byte. If all ten spaces are used, a zero byte must be present in location 042C. The following location contains the automatically-entered backspace character, normally a ^H (08h). If your printer uses a different code for backspacing, you will want to change this entry.

HIGH-ORDER BIT USAGE IN WORDSTAR

Except for the opening 31 control codes, the first 127 characters of the complete ASCII character set are considered to comprise the normal printable subset. The binary equivalents of these characters require only seven bits, leaving the eighth (the leftmost or high-order bit) a zero. In WordStar these high-order bits are used in text for special purposes: 1) to designate "soft" characters, and 2) to mark the ends of words subject to microjustification. (They are also used in menus and messages to designate highlighted characters and spaces.) When set, the high-order bit is changed from 0 to 1.

So-called soft characters are those which are inserted by word-wrap, paragraph reforming, and hyphenation operations—and are thus subject to change in subsequent editing operations. They are formed by adding 80h to the hex values of their "hard" counterparts (which are not subject to these changes) and include soft carriage returns (8Dh), line feeds (8Ah), hyphens (ADh), and spaces (A0h).

In actuality, setting the high-order bit converts a character in the lower half of the ASCII set to one in the upper half. WordStar internally manipulates these bits or strips them before sending characters to the PC's monitor, so the modified characters display like ordinary text characters. They are present in text files produced in document mode, however, which you can verify by examining these files with Norton's DiskLook (in hex display) or SecMod program. You can also scan them by using the Type command in DOS. Ordinarily all this is of limited practical consequence, but it can become important if you want to read WordStar files with another program, transmit them, or display them on another device.

Many programs and devices ignore high-order bits, and their presence causes no difficulties, but that is not always true. A way of avoiding the problem entirely is, where practical, to use the non-document mode. In this mode no high-order bits are set, with one important exception: **using the paragraph reform command, ^B, causes high-order bits to be set, even in non-document mode.** Moreover, their presence will not be evident on screen since no visible effect takes place. If you are unsure whether high-order bits are present in a file and if they make a difference, check the file with SecMod or the Type command.

ADDRESS LISTINGS

Table 11-1 lists addresses, standard unmodified values, functions, and appropriate notes for items discussed here, as well as a few for which no discussion was felt to be necessary. If you have a copy of the USER-1 notes from an earlier WordStar manual, you may notice that it contains certain items not present here. Most of these have to do with specialized console routines not applicable to the IBM PC; in the interests of brevity and minimum "noise" they were left out. Others apply but in a practical sense are not modifiable. Such omissions account for whatever gaps are present in address sequences.

Table 11-1. Addresses Of Selected Functions

Addr	*Std-Val*	*Function And Notes*
0248	18	Screen height in lines (24; see text)
0249	50	Screen width in columns (80)
		* * * * * *
02CF	01	DEL1 Cursor blink control (''on'' time)
02D0	04	DEL2 Cursor blink control (''off'' time)
02D1	08	DEL3 Medium-long Delay
02D2	16	DEL4 Long Delay
02D3	09	DEL5 Redisplay Delay
02D6	FF	MS/PC-DOS. Set 00 for CP/M-86
02DC	01	Default disk; 01 = A:, 02 = B:, etc.
02DD	14	Horiz scroll overlap (std = 20 columns)
02E0 through 035B		User patch area. Check carefully; may be used by Install program.
		* * * * *
0422	00 00 00 00	Automatic backspace table (see text
0426	00 00 00 00	for discussion)
042A	00 00	
042C	00	Terminates above if table is filled.
042D	08	Backspace code for above; change if your printer requires another.

Appendix A

CHARACTER AND NUMBER CONVERSIONS

All data associated with WordStar are represented in memory in a form of notation known as hexadecimal or, for convenience, simply hex. Control codes, commands, messages, and numeric values all must be converted from their more familiar alphabetic or decimal form to hex whenever you make a patch to a program. This is undeniably a nuisance, but it is not difficult and can be done strictly by rote if you prefer. Some programs allow you to use decimal equivalents for ASCII characters, but you must still look them up in a table as will be done here.

Because it differs from our ingrained way of thinking about numbers, hex notation can seem confusing at first, but it is really simpler than it looks. Hex numbers are based on a system of 16 units (0 through F) rather than the 10 units (0 through 9) of our more familiar decimal system. The basic relationship is as follows:

Decimal	0 . . . 9	10	11	12	13	14	15	16 . . .
Hexadecimal	0 . . . 9	A	B	C	D	E	F	10 . . .

The numbers 0 through 9 are the same in both systems, but from 10 on they are different. In the decimal system we represent 10 with not one digit but two. Put another way, we have one group of ten and no units—or we have exchanged ten pennies for a dime. But in hex a dime is equivalent not to 10 pennies but 16. Since we have no way of uniquely representing the added six units with single numerals, we use letters as substitutes.

Mentally converting numbers from decimal to hex is unhandy, especially as the numbers grow larger. Table A-1 is a useful conversion chart. Some inexpensive scientific calculators, like the Sharp model EL-560H, have hex conversion capability and simplify handling even large numbers.

You may wonder why we use such a scheme in the first place. The reason is that our decimal system is not efficient with computers, which use binary arithmetic at the machine operations level. The hexadecimal system is more compatible since 16 is a power of 2, the binary base, while 10 is not. Each group of four binary bits translates to a single hex digit. Hexadecimal is thus a good middle ground between the machine and its users.

To prevent confusion between decimal and hex numbers the latter often are written with a trailing letter h (21h or 21H, for example) unless the context makes it clear which is intended. Do not include the letter h or H, however, when making an actual patch.

Direct number conversions from decimal to hex apply when dealing with an actual quantity or value rather than a symbolic representation of another entity, such as a control code or other character. An example of this is page length expressed in number of lines. The standard default value of 66 lines is converted to hex and entered as 42.

Control codes, alphabetic characters, and numerals are represented by a special set of codes known as the American Standard Code for Information Interchange or, more simply, ASCII (pronounced "askey"). The complete ASCII character set consists of 256 characters, of which we are interested mainly in the first half, since most printers—especially daisy-wheelers—can only print this half, minus the control codes.

Table A-2 shows conversions from ASCII characters to their hexadecimal and binary equivalents. Each ASCII character is represented by two hex digits. The first two columns contain control codes, denoted as such by a leading caret (^). Note that each of the control codes contains a second entry below, such as a CR (for carriage return) below the Control-M. These second entries are the commonly used abbreviations for communications and printer control codes. Their hex values are exactly the same as their control-letter counterparts. (Note: For personal use and convenience, you can make photocopies of tables A-1 and A-2 and put them in a clear plastic holder or have them laminated for protection.)

To convert an ASCII character to its hexadecimal equivalent, first find the character in the table. At the top of that column in bold type is the first hex digit. The second hex digit is to the right of the character at the end of the row and is also in bold. The hex equivalent of a Control-O, for example, is 0F. A capital O is 4F. A numeral 6 is equivalent to 36h. You may note that any arabic numeral, 0 through 9, can be represented in hex by simply preceding it with a 3.

Although you will seldom need them, binary values are included in the table. To convert an ASCII character or its hex equivalent to binary, begin with the bits above the first hex digit and follow them with the equivalent bits for the second digit. The binary value for a capital O or hex 4F, for example, is 1001111. (Although eight bits are used for each character in the full ASCII set, the subset shown here uses only seven. The eighth, the leftmost or high-order bit, is normally a zero, but WordStar uses it for special purposes including character highlighting.)

Regarding binary numbers, there is a potentially confusing aspect of table A-2 relating to bit numbering. In ASCII the rightmost (low-order) bit customarily is referred to as bit one. Otherwise, programmers and engineers usually refer to the low-order position as bit zero, a practice followed in technical literature like the IBM Technical Reference Manual. This is not often a concern in WordStar but is worth remembering. If you encounter it and become confused (easy to do), just forget labeled bit positions and count left from the rightmost bit.

Table A-1. Decimal To Hexadecimal Conversion

Dec	Hex	Dec	Hex	Dec	Hex	Dec	Hex	Dec	Hex
1	1	41	29	81	51	121	79	161	A1
2	2	42	2A	82	52	122	7A	162	A2
3	3	43	2B	83	53	123	7B	163	A3
4	4	44	2C	84	54	124	7C	164	A4
5	5	45	2D	85	55	125	7D	165	A5
6	6	46	2E	86	56	126	7E	166	A6
7	7	47	2F	87	57	127	7F	167	A7
8	8	48	30	88	58	128	80	168	A8
9	9	49	31	89	59	129	81	169	A9
10	A	50	32	90	5A	130	82	170	AA
11	B	51	33	91	5B	131	83	171	AB
12	C	52	34	92	5C	132	84	172	AC
13	D	53	35	93	5D	133	85	173	AD
14	E	54	36	94	5E	134	86	174	AE
15	F	55	37	95	5F	135	87	175	AF
16	10	56	38	96	60	136	88	176	B0
17	11	57	39	97	61	137	89	177	B1
18	12	58	3A	98	62	138	8A	178	B2
19	13	59	3B	99	63	139	8B	179	B3
20	14	60	3C	100	64	140	8C	180	B4
21	15	61	3D	101	65	141	8D	181	B5
22	16	62	3E	102	66	142	8E	182	B6
23	17	63	3F	103	67	143	8F	183	B7
24	18	64	40	104	68	144	90	184	B8
25	19	65	41	105	69	145	91	185	B9
26	1A	66	42	106	6A	146	92	186	BA
27	1B	67	43	107	6B	147	93	187	BB
28	1C	68	44	108	6C	148	94	188	BC
29	1D	69	45	109	6D	149	95	189	BD
30	1E	70	46	110	6E	150	96	190	BE
31	1F	71	47	111	6F	151	97	191	BF
32	20	72	48	112	70	152	98	192	C0
33	21	73	49	113	71	153	99	193	C1
34	22	74	4A	114	72	154	9A	194	C2
35	23	75	4B	115	73	155	9B	195	C3
36	24	76	4C	116	74	156	9C	196	C4
37	25	77	4D	117	75	157	9D	197	C5
38	26	78	4E	118	76	158	9E	198	C6
39	27	79	4F	119	77	159	9F	199	C7
40	28	80	50	120	78	160	A0	200	C8

Table A-2. ASCII To Hex And Binary Conversion

000 **0**	001 **1**	010 **2** (A)*	011 **3** (B)*	100 **4** (C)*	101 **5** (D)*	110 **6** (E)*	111 **7** (F)*	←bits 7,6,5 ←1st Hex Digit ↓ 2nd Digit	bits 4-1
Null	^P DLE	space	0	@	P	‘	p	**0**	0000
^A SOH	^Q DC1	!	1	A	Q	a	q	**1**	0001
^B STX	^R DC2	"	2	B	R	b	r	**2**	0010
^C ETX	^S DC3	#	3	C	S	c	s	**3**	0011
^D EOT	^T DC4	$	4	D	T	d	t	**4**	0100
^E ENQ	^U NAC	%	5	E	U	e	u	**5**	0101
^F ACK	^V SYN	&	6	F	V	f	v	**6**	0110
^G BEL	^W ETB	’	7	G	W	g	w	**7**	0111
^H BS	^X CAN	(	8	H	X	h	x	**8**	1000
^I HT	^Y EM	)	9	I	Y	i	y	**9**	1001
^J LF	^Z SUB	*	:	J	Z	j	z	**A**	1010
^K VT	ESC	+	;	K	[	k	{	**B**	1011
^L FF	^\\ FS	,	<	L	\\	l	|	**C**	1100
^M CR	^] GS	–	=	M	]	m	}	**D**	1101
^N SO	^6 RS	.	>	N	^	n	~	**E**	1110
^O SI	^_ US	/	?	O	_	o	Del	**F**	1111

* Hex prefix for highlighted characters (i.e. 41 = A; C1 = A highlighted) Applies only to WordStar.

Appendix B

A BASIC UTILITY PROGRAM FOR PRINTED DUMPS

For readers who have at least a passing familiarity with Basic, listed here is a simple program for producing printed dumps. Intended primarily for use with WordStar, it is handy for dumping other files also, either in its existing form or with a slight change (omit line 340) which eliminates conversion of high-bit characters (as in WordStar menus) to normal printing characters. Although limited to files not larger than 32K, it produces printed output in the same format that Debug produces on-screen and is a useful adjunct to Debug as a reference and modification tool.

You can use Basic to get the program into executable form, but an even easier way is to use the non-document mode (N) in WordStar. Just be sure to enter it as shown, without any extraneous characters. Observe the comments regarding spaces, since they affect printed output format. You can omit the comments themselves if you wish.

When you finish entering the program and verify the accuracy of your input, save it to disk as DUMP.BAS. For ease in use, copy it to your DOS diskette or your working copy of WordStar, along with BASIC or BASICA in the latter case. Invoke the program by entering **basic dump** at the DOS prompt. When loaded, the program prompts you to turn your printer on and enter the drive and name of the file to dump (follow DOS rules). If the file is on the logged drive, you can omit the drive letter. As written, the program prints on fan-fold paper; it does not pause between pages.

An advanced file dump program is available on diskette with manual from Exicom, Inc., P.O. Box 831951, Richardson, TX, 75083. Called **Dump2**, it has several menu-driven features, allows you to select and dump any part of a file, handles file sizes up to one megabyte, and is much faster. Its price is $24.50 postpaid in North America. (Texas residents add $1.50 sales tax.)

```
100 '       * * * DUMP.BAS - Printed Dump Utility * * *
110 DEFINT A-Z : CLS : CLOSE : PRINT : PRINT
120 PRINT "Program ready - Turn your printer ON" : PRINT
130 INPUT "Enter drive and file name: ",FILE$ : PRINT
140 OPEN "R",#1,FILE$
150 FIELD #1,128 AS RCD$
160 OPEN "lpt1:" FOR OUTPUT AS #2
170 PRINT "Now dumping file . . . Press Ctrl-Break to stop."
180 PRINT #2, "          File dump of "+FILE$+" . . ."
190 PRINT #2,""
200 OFST = 256
210 BIN1$ = ""
220 BIN2$ = ""
230 FOR B=1 TO 6
240    GET #1
250    IF EOF(1) THEN 420
260    PRINT #2, SPC(14);
270    PRINT #2, "0 1 2 3  4 5 6 7  8 9 A B  C D E F"
280    FOR I=1 TO LEN(RCD$)
290      CHAR = ASC(MID$(RCD$,I,1))
300      CHAR$ = HEX$(CHAR)
310      IF LEN(CHAR$)=1 THEN CHAR$="0"+CHAR$
320      BIN1$=BIN1$+CHAR$
330      NPCHAR$ = "."
340      IF (CHAR > 160) AND (CHAR < 255) THEN CHAR=CHAR-128
350      IF (CHAR < 32) OR (CHAR > 126) THEN 370
360      NPCHAR$ = CHR$(CHAR)
370      BIN2$ = BIN2$ + NPCHAR$
380      IF LEN(BIN1$) = 32 THEN GOSUB 470
390    NEXT I
400 NEXT B
410 LPRINT CHR$(12) : GOTO 230
420 GOSUB 470
430 CLOSE
440 PRINT : PRINT "File Dump Complete"
450 LPRINT CHR$(12) : LPRINT CHR$(13)
460 END
470 RECLEN = LEN(BIN1$)
480 IF RECLEN = 0 THEN 620
490 OFST$="    "+HEX$(OFST)                  '4 spaces between quotes
500 OFST$=MID$(OFST$,LEN(OFST$)-4,5)
510 PRINT #2, SPC(6);
520 PRINT #2,OFST$+":  ";                    '2 spaces after colon
```

```
530 J=1
540    IF RECLEN-J < 8 THEN 580
550    PRINT #2,MID$(BIN1$,J,8)+" ";          '1 space between quotes
560    J = J+8
570    GOTO 540
580 PRINT #2,MID$(BIN1$,J) + "  [" + BIN2$ + "]"
590 OFST = OFST + RECLEN/2
600 BIN1$ = ""                                 '2 spaces before first
610 BIN2$ = ""                                 'bracket in line 580
620 RETURN
```

Appendix C

SUPPLEMENT FOR CP/M-80 VERSIONS

Users of 8-bit computers and the CP/M operating system generally have good reason to feel forsaken by software developers in the stampede to DOS and 16-bit machines. Happily for the still numerous users of the former, this is not true of WordStar. Although perhaps at a less aggressive level than before, support for CP/M versions has continued, and the purpose of this section is to provide a bridge to those versions.

Because of the variety of 8-bit machines in the field, there can be differences in certain WordStar-to-hardware interfaces, for instance those involving monitors. Some use memory-mapped video and some do not; others may use unusual terminal or printer drivers. Variations are more likely to be present when WordStar is supplied by a manufacturer who bundles hardware and software. Some of these are, or were, straight generic versions, but others may be factory-customized to one degree or another. While it is not feasible here to identify and cover such differences in detail, they affect relatively few of the functions we are interested in.

Although material in this book centers on IBM and compatible versions of WordStar operating under DOS, most of it applies to CP/M-80 versions as well. The main differences are in memory addresses and the presence or absence of certain fields or tables, such as those for function keys and cursor control keys. To serve as a baseline, address data is provided for two widely used CP/M-80 versions of WordStar: 3.0, released in 1981, and 3.3, released in 1983. Included in tables at the end of this section are labels or other identifiers which correlate with functional explanations in the preceding chapters. With this material and a printed dump of the first 900 or so locations from your working copy of WS.COM, you should be able to identify, understand, and operate successfully on a large majority of the modifiable features within WordStar.

Subject headings that follow relate to corresponding chapters in the main part of this book. To avoid repetition, material presented here is confined to that applying specifically to CP/M-80 versions of the program. It is recommended that you read these related chapters in conjunction with information found here. This will make modifications easier by helping you acquire an overall understanding of structure, format, and operation of the functions you wish to customize.

Although all examples and specific patches presented in this book have been tested and verified on PC-DOS versions of WordStar, tests on CP/M-80 versions were necessarily limited. Given the variety of existing machines and program versions, you could occasionally have a problem when adapting a modification to your particular hardware-software environment. If this occurs, check carefully that addresses and examples given here apply to your setup. If not, you may have to seek more information on machine interfaces. As a last resort, you can always return to the original form.

GETTING STARTED (Chapter 2)

Organization and overall structure of CP/M-80 versions of WordStar are substantially the same as for DOS. That is, the three main programs are WS.COM, WSOVLY1.OVR, and WSMSGS.OVR. Within each of these, content is similar except that certain functions present in DOS versions are absent in CP/M-80 versions, and the order may differ slightly. Differences in WS.COM are detailed in the address listings at the end of this section. **Always be careful not to confuse WordStar 3.3 for DOS with version 3.3 for CP/M-80.** This may seem obvious, but it is an easy mistake to make when you are more intent on the modifications themselves.

The comments made about WSOVLY1 apply generally to CP/M-80 versions as well; there is little of interest in this program in a customizing sense. Comments about the Messages program apply also, but file contents may differ somewhat, particularly in the number of menu versions present. Differences can be readily identified in a printed dump or with your debugger program, since nearly all of this file is in plain text.

Your debugger program may be labeled DDT or SID in the directory on your CP/M diskette. In general these programs operate much like Debug in DOS, and the on-screen displays are essentially the same. Unless you are already versed in using the debugger, however, it is recommended that you read appropriate portions of your CP/M operating system manual.

A printed dump of locations 0100 through 0900 of WS.COM is especially recommended as a tool for comparing your particular version of WordStar with the address listings in this book. You can produce one easily by following the general technique described in Chapter 2 using the Dump command in DDT or SID and the applicable screen-to-printer command.

Again, refer to your CP/M operating system manual if you are not sure how to do this.

To determine whether addresses given here are appropriate for your version of WordStar, compare your printed dump with the listings at the end of this section. Look for clues revealed by formats and character sequences as described in the preceding chapters and noted in the address listings. Operating default areas, for example, are generally easy to spot since you will see a succession of FF and 00 entries interspersed with numeric values for defaults requiring such. Command tables are characterized by patterns that repeat themselves every few bytes, the number depending on format. In most cases it will not be necessary to engage in this level of deciphering, but learning the landmarks will help you become comfortable at finding your way around in WS.COM.

Keep in mind that the exact characters you find at a given location in your program may differ from those shown, if any, in tables and examples. As mentioned earlier, there can be variations based on machine type and installation parameters. If you find such differences and are not sure why they exist, it is best to investigate before proceeding with a patch.

FUNCTION KEYS AND CURSOR CONTROLS (Chapter 3)

In the CP/M-80 universe, function keys are handled differently from DOS versions of WordStar. In general, there is no built-in WordStar support for such keys. This is not to say, however, that function keys cannot be used with 8-bit versions of the program. Some machines have built-in function key capabilities, often in firmware (ROM, etc.). In such cases, these keys may be programmable with WordStar commands, but this facility exists outside WordStar. As far as the latter is concerned, it sees these commands in the same form as if you had typed standard command characters at the keyboard. Your ability to change function key assignments is thus governed by whatever provisions exist in the basic machine.

Somewhere you might encounter a factory-customized CP/M-80 version of WordStar with some form of function key support, but this would be uncommon. In this event, format is the clue to locating addresses. In general you would find a length byte, usually in the range of 01 to 06, followed by a control character in the range of 01 to 1A, which in turn would be followed by other ASCII characters. Any unused bytes in the field normally would be filled with asterisks (2Ah). This pattern would be repeated for as many keys as are supported. As you may suspect, poking around in WS.COM without a roadmap can lead to strange places, so be cautious about changes.

If your computer is an Osborne Executive model, there is another way of dealing with function keys as well as numerous other features of value to WordStar users. It involves a program called SKEYS, which is fast, easy to use, and has attributes of both a keyboard enhancer and a desktop utility such as Borland's Sidekick. Once loaded, it sits unobtrusively in the background, like a genie awaiting its master's call. It is available from Inova, 11311 Stemmons Frwy, Suite 7, Dallas, TX, 75229.

EDITING AND FILE COMMANDS (Chapter 4)

You can modify editing and file commands using the same techniques described in the related chapter covering the IBM PC. In fact, addresses for the No-File (Opening) and editing command tables for CP/M-80 version 3.0 of WordStar are the same as for IBM versions. However, this is not true of merge-print commands, pointers, and special character tables. Nor is it true for CP/M-80 version 3.3; to be safe, refer to tables at the end of this section. Remember that often there are slight but important differences in the order of entries and their locations from one release to another.

ON-SCREEN DISPLAYS AND MESSAGES (Chapter 5)

Monitor interfaces in WordStar often differ from one machine model to another. In versions for the IBM PC and compatibles there are special terminal driver routines which simplify modification of on-screen display characteristics. Although routines for other computers are conceptually similar, implementations may differ considerably. In addition to IVON and IVOFF functions, they often involve unique control strings to insert and delete lines, erase to end of line, and so on. There can be more complexity as well. Although WordStar provides for these functions in software, it also allows for more direct machine paths. The latter usually result in faster operation and therefore are often used, but it makes the interface more machine-dependent. Unless you have a good working knowledge of all this or have access to someone who does, it is best to leave display attributes as they are.

You can modify menus and messages with relative impunity and with many useful results. The same basic techniques apply as are discussed for the IBM PC. When changing the contents of menus, you may find it helpful to prepare a printed dump of those sections of WSMSGS, even though they appear in plain text. This is good procedure for two reasons. In the case of menus, it will help you identify the proper menu when multiple versions are present. In all cases it will help you get back to the original form if you make a mistake and have to start over.

Your debugger may require that WSMSGS.OVR be redesignated as a .COM file to be loadable. If so, copy the debugger program and the messages file to a blank, formatted diskette, rename the messages file, and proceed with the printed dump as outlined earlier.

START-UP AND OPERATING DEFAULTS (Chapter 6)

As true of IBM versions, settings for start-up and operating defaults in your version of WordStar can have considerable influence on operating convenience and productivity. Although many of these are accessible by keyboard command, you can avoid the lost time and bother of constantly massaging them by setting up the program so that it comes up automatically the way you want it. If you need the flexibility of more than one WordStar configuration to handle different writing tasks, you can create multiple program diskettes, each set up for a specific application.

Later CP/M-80 versions of WordStar included Install programs that give you access to more functions via the installation menu, but numerous other functions still can be modified only by patching. You generally have the option of doing this by using the patcher facility in the installation program, but you may find, as others have, that using your debugger is often faster and more convenient.

In general you will find that the formats and operational descriptions covered in Chapter 6 apply to your version as well. Addresses, of course, may be different; check the listings at the end of this section. It is always a good idea to verify addresses, formats, and character sequences by comparing data presented here against a printed dump of your installed, working copy of the program.

USING PRINTERS (Chapter 9)

Of all modifiable sections of WordStar, the printer patch area may be the most useful to users of CP/M-80 versions. Waves of new and improved printers of all types have appeared on the market since the last program update was released, and many of the old workhorses on the printer menu have been superseded by faster, more versatile models. Although you obviously will not find these printers on the installation menu, this need not deter you from installing and using one to full advantage.

Even if you do not plan to change printers, information presented here will help you extract more performance from your present machine. As in DOS versions, standard installation routines seldom exploit all capabilities of your printer, especially if it is a dot matrix model.

Apart from address differences, printer controls and functions closely follow those described in Chapter 9 with few exceptions. In rare instances you might encounter POSMTH values of 03 or 04. These were used with special OEM printers and may involve unique software drivers, which affects values of CSWTCH as well. They were associated mostly with early program releases, and there probably are few remaining in use. If you are still using one of these antique setups, a general upgrade may be in order.

Depending on your specific hardware and operating system configuration, you may or may not have to use mode and redirect commands when driving a serial printer. Consult your hardware and operating system manuals for this information. Check the value of CSWTCH as well. If your operating system permits defining a serial port as the primary list device, 00 should work; otherwise try 04. Another approach is to run Install for a similar printer listed on the menu, specifying it as a serial printer. The value inserted for CSWTCH should be correct for your printer also.

PROPORTIONAL SPACING (Chapter 10)

Since proportionally spaced printing is in most respects a function of printer characteristics, requiring a printer having microspacing capability, this chapter applies to CP/M-80 versions generally as it stands. Checks of 3.0 and 3.3 have not revealed the table errors present in DOS versions, so you can forget about the related patches. If you are so inclined, however, improvements in print quality may be realized by optimizing spacing values for your particular setup using the techniques described. In particular, check values for lower case letters m, w, l, and i. It is also worth trying different width values in text, such as .CW9 for a proportional wheel.

Remember that the ASCII display section of your debugger translates width values in the spacing table as if they were characters, but this is meaningless. WordStar relates width values to characters by their positions in the table. The ASCII display section is useful, however, in helping you find the spacing table in program versions not listed.

OTHER MODIFICATIONS (Chapter 11)

With appropriate changes of addresses the discussions of display timing parameters (DEL1 through DEL5), default disk drive (DEFDSK), horizontal scrolling distance (SCRLSZ), automatic backspace table (AUTOBS), and high-order bit usage apply to CP/M-80 versions. Modifications to the version 3.3 function key display apply only to DOS versions of the program.

ADDRESS LISTINGS

Table C-1 lists labels, addresses, and brief functional descriptions for CP/M-80 WordStar versions 3.0 and 3.3. A cross reference to equivalent IBM addresses is included to help you find related discussions and details about specific functions in preceding chapters.

Version 3.0 information is based on MicroPro's generic technical data. Addresses for version 3.3 are based on releases for the Osborne Executive but agree closely with those for Kaypro machines also. Nonetheless, be on the lookout for differences in the WordStar release for your machine.

The best way to do this is to mark up a printed dump of appropriate sections of WS.COM for your particular release. You can use a straightedge to rule off the beginning and end of each section, i.e. the sections where all ^K commands (hex 0B), ^Q commands (hex 11), and so forth are located. Since many fields are repetitive and fixed in length, such as four bytes, you can use vertical rules to set off each field. Once you have accurately identified a reference point, you will often find that everything lines up in neat, geometric patterns. All this may seem laborious at first, but it need be done only once and will produce a valuable reference.

Table C-2 lists individual addresses of width values and the character with which each is associated for versions 3.0 and 3.3 of CP/M-80 WordStar. See related comments in this section and details in Chapter 10.

Table C-1. WS.COM Addresses For CP/M-80 Versions Of WordStar With PC-DOS Cross Reference

Label	*3.3 DOS*	*3.0 CP/M-80*	*3.3 CP/M-80*	*Function*
		* * * Screen Height And Width * * *		
HITE	0248	0248	0232	Screen height in lines
WID	0249	0249	0233	Screen width in columns
		* * * Term/monitor Interface (see text) * * *		
ERAEOL	026D	026D	0250	Erase to end of line
LINDEL	0274	0274	0257	Delete line
LININS	027B	027B	025E	Insert line
IVON	0284	0284	0267	Highlighting on
IVOFF	028B	028B	026E	Highlighting off
IBMATT	02D5	n/a	n/a	Attribute byte (IBM only)
TRMINI	0292	0292	0275	Initialize terminal
TRMUNI	029B	029B	027E	Un-initialize terminal
INISUB	02A4	02A4	0287	Jump to alt term init subrt
UNISUB	02A7	02A7	028A	Jump to alt un-init subrt
USELST	02AA	02AA	028D	Antiscroll flag (last row/col)
DELCUS	02AE	02AE	028E	Delay after cursor pos (msec)
DELMIS	02AF	02AF	028F	Miscellaneous delay (msec)
MEMAPV	02B0	02B0	0290	FF = memory-mapped video
MEMADR	02B1	02B1	0291	Home addr for above (2 bytes)
HIBIV	02B3	02B3	0293	FF = highlight by high bit
HIBCUR	02B4	02B4	0294	FF = show cursor by high bit
CRBLIV	02B5	02B5	0295	FF = WS blinks cursor
ZAFCIN	02B6	02B6	0296	Zero after character input
RUBFXF	02B8	02B8	0298	FF = use RFIXER
RFIXER	02B9	02B9	0299	Char to output after 'delete'
		* * * Display Timing, Disk Control, Scrolling * * *		
DEL1	02CF	O2CF	02AF	'On' time of cursor blink
DEL2	02D0	02D0	02B0	'Off' time of cursor blink
DEL3	02D1	02D1	02B1	Delay until menu scrolls down
DEL4	02D2	02D2	02B2	Time sign-on, msgs stay on scr
DEL5	02D3	02D3	02B3	Del to rewrite scr on hor scrl
RSTFLG	02DB	02DB	n/a	FF = no disk resets
DEFDSK	02DC	02DC	02B9	Default drive for WS pgm files
SCRLSZ	02DD	02DD	02BA	Overlap on horiz scroll (col's)
MORPAT	02E0	02E0	02CB	Start of user subrt patch area

Table C-1. WS.COM Addresses For CP/M-80 Versions Of WordStar (Continued)

Label	*3.3 DOS*	*3.0 CP/M-80*	*3.3 CP/M-80*	*Function*
		* * * Initial And Operating Defaults * * *		
ITHELP	0360	0360	034D	Initial help level
NITHLF	0361	0361	034E	Start-up help msg, on/off
ITITOG	0362	0362	034F	Insert mode, on/off
ITDSDR	0363	0363	0350	Initial file dir, on/off
		* * * Page Formatting * * *		
INITPF	0366	0366	0351	
	0367	0367	0352	
	0368	0368	0353	
	036A	036A	0355	Initial
	036B	036B	0356	
	036C	036C	0357	Page
	036E	036E	0359	
	036F	036F	035A	Formatting
	0370	0370	035B	
	0372	0372	035D	Defaults
	0373	0373	035E	
	0374	0374	035F	——
	0376	0376	0361	
	0377	0377	0362	See
	0378	0378	0363	
	037A	037A	0365	Chapter 6
	037B	037B	0366	
	037C	037C	0367	
	037D	037D	0368	
	037E	037E	0369	
		* * * Margin Settings And S'script Roll * * *		
INITLM	037F	037F	036A	Initial left margin, -1
INITRM	0380	0380	036B	Initial right margin, -1
INITSR	0381	0381	036C	Initial sub/superscript roll
		* * * Initial Editing Defaults * * *		
ITITWF	0385	0385	036D	Word-wrap, on/off
	0386	0386	036E	Justification, on/off
	0387	0387	036F	Variable tabs, on/off

Table C-1. WS.COM Addresses For CP/M-80 Versions Of WordStar (Continued)

Label	3.3 DOS	3.0 CP/M-80	3.3 CP/M-80	Function	
	0388	0388	0370	Soft hyphens, on/off	
	0389	0389	0371	Hyphen help, on/off	
	038A	038A	0372	Display format chars	
	038B	038B	0373	Display ruler line	
	038C	038C	0374	Collect page-break data	
	038D	038D	0375	Display page breaks	
	038E	038E	0376	Line spacing	
	038F	038F	0377	Block move mode	
NONDOC	0392	0392	0378	File opening mode	
DECCHR	0393	0393	037A	Decimal tab align char	
		* * * Dot Commands And Print Formatting * * *			
DOTCHR	0395	0395	037B	Dot command, initial char	
BLNCHR	0396	0396	0386	Non-break space char	
CMTCHR	n/a	n/a	0387	Comment char (; or 3Bh)	
ENDEXP	n/a	n/a	0388	G (47h)	
DOTSON	0397	0397	0379	Enable dot command display	
		* * * Hyphenation Criteria * * *			
HZONE	039A	039A	03C9	Length of hyphen zone (col's)	
	039B	039B	03CA	Address of special vowel table	
	039D	039D	03CC	Address of regular vowel table	
VOWTAB	039F	039F	03CE	10 bytes (see Chap 6)	
		* * * Special Characters Displayed While Editing * * *			
EOFCHR	03AD	03AD	03DF	End-of-file char	(.)
BOFCHR	03AE	03AE	03DD	Begin-of-file char	(:)
CONCHR	03AF	03AF	03DE	Line exceeds scr width	(+)
OVPCHR	03B0	03B0	03E3	Next line overprint	(−)
LFCHR	03B1	03B1	03E2	Line ends in LF only	J
PAGCHR	03B2	03B2	03E4	Line is last of page	P
SOFTCR	03B3	03B3	03E5	Line ends in soft CR	( )
HARDCR	03B4	03B4	03E1	Line ends in hard CR	<
FDTCHR	03B5	03B5	03E0	Line has Merge dot cmnd	M
SOFHYC	03B8	03B8	03E7	Soft hyphen char	(ADh)
PAGFIL	03B9	03B9	03E8	Char for page-brk line	(−)
MARKS	03BA	03BA	03E9	Char for Begin-Blk mkr	B
	03BB	03BB	03EA	Char for End-Blk mkr	K
	03BC	03BC	03EB	Intrnl mkr - Do not change	

Table C-1. WS.COM Addresses For CP/M-80 Versions Of WordStar (Continued)

Label	*3.3 DOS*	*3.0 CP/M-80*	*3.3 CP/M-80*	*Function*	
	03BD	03BD	03EC	Intrnl mkr - Do not change	
	03BE	03BE	03ED	Internal mkr - Unused	
	03BF	03BF	03EE	Text-place mkrs, 10 bytes	
		* * * Defaults For Printing Options * * *			
PODBLK	03CA	03CA	03F8	Disk File Output? Y/N	
	03CB	03CB	03F9	Use Form Feeds? Y/N	
	03CC	03CC	03FA	Suppr Page Format'g? Y/N	
	03CD	03CD	03FB	Pause Betwn Pages? Y/N	
NOUFF	03D1	03D1	03FC	Show "Use Form Feeds?"	
ITPOPN	03D3	03D3	03FD	Omit std page numbers	
ITMIJ	03D4	03D4	03FE	.UJ dot command enable	
ITBIP	03D5	03D5	03FF	Bidirectional pntg enable	
RVELIM	03D8	03D8	0389	MM-Data value separator	(,)
RVQUOT	03D9	03D9	038A	MM-Delimiter	(")
VARCH1	03DB	03DB	038E	MM-Char to begin variable	(&)
VARCH2	03DC	03DC	038F	MM-Char to end variable	(&)
VARNBC	03DD	03DD	n/a	MM-Char to omit line	(obsol.)
VAROPC	03DE	03DE	0390	MM-Separator for optn ltrs	(/)
	03DF	03DF	0391	MM-Omit line if vbl null	(O)
COMPOP	n/a	n/a	0396	MM-Compar oprs	3C 3E 00 FD 3E
LOGICP	n/a	n/a	03B7	MM-Logic oprs	2C 41 4E 44 2E
		* * * Program File Names * * *			
FNWSCM	03E6	03E6	0400	WS COM	preserve
DSKTNA	03F2	03F2	040C	WSMSGS OVR	format
FNOVLY	03FE	03FE	0418	WSOVLY1 OVR	——
FNMRGP	040A	040A	0424	MAILMRGEOVR	see Chap 6
		* * * Opening Menu (No-File) Commands * * *			
NOFTAB	0430	0430	043C	Open document file	^D
	0434	0434	0440	Open non-document file	^N
	0438	0438	0444	Set help level	^H
	043C	043C	0448	Exit to system (DOS)	^X
	0440	0440	044C	Print a file	^P
	0444	0444	0450	Initiate Merge-Print	^M
	0448	0448	0454	Delete a file	^Y
	044C	044C	0458	File directory on-off	^F
	0450	0450	045C	Scroll directory up	^Z

Table C-1. WS.COM Addresses For CP/M-80 Versions Of WordStar (Continued)

Label	3.3 DOS	3.0 CP/M-80	3.3 CP/M-80	Function	
	0454	0454	0460	Scroll directory down	^W
	0458	0458	0464	Change logged drive	^L
	045C	045C	0468	Run a program	^R
	0460	0460	046C	Copy a file	^O
	0464	0464	0470	Rename a file	^E
	046C	046C	0478	Run Spell/CorrectStar	^S
		* * * Editing Commands * * *			
VTAB	0481	0481	0489	Prefix for Quick menu	^Q
	0485	0485	048C	Prefix for Block menu	^K
	0489	0489	0491	Prefix On-screen menu	^O
	048D	048D	0495	Prefix for Help menu	^J
	0491	0491	0499	Set help level	^J ^H
	0495	0495	049C	Cursor left character	^S
	0499	0499	04A1	Alternate for above	Bkspc
	049D	049D	04A5	Cursor right character	^D
	04A1	04A1	04A9	Cursor left word	^A
	04A5	04A5	04AC	Cursor right word	^F
	04A9	04A9	04B1	Cursor down line	^X
	04AD	04AD	04B5	Cursor up line	^E
	04B1	04B1	04B9	Cursor lft side of scr	^Q ^S
	04B5	04B5	04BC	Cursor rt end-of-line	^Q ^D
	04B9	04B9	04C1	Cursor bottom of screen	^Q ^X
	04BD	04BD	04C5	Cursor top of screen	^Q ^E
	04C1	04C1	04C9	Cursor to block begin	^QB
	04C5	04C5	04CC	Cursor to block end	^QK
	04C9	04C9	04D1	Cursor to prev pos	^QP
	04CD	04CD	04D5	Cursor to last find/rpl	^QV
	04D1	04D1	04D9	Cursor to marker zero	^Q0
	04D5	04D5	04DC	Cursor to marker one	^Q1
	04D9	04D9	04E1	Cursor to marker two	^Q2
	04DD	04DD	04E5	Cursor to marker three	^Q3
	04E1	04E1	04E9	Cursor to marker four	^Q4
	04E5	04E5	04EC	Cursor to marker five	^Q5
	04E9	04E9	04F1	Cursor to marker six	^Q6
	04ED	04ED	04F5	Cursor to marker seven	^Q7
	04F1	04F1	04F9	Cursor to marker eight	^Q8
	04F5	04F5	04FC	Cursor to marker nine	^Q9
	04F9	04F9	0501	Cursor to begin-of-file	^Q ^R
	04FD	04FD	0505	Cursor to end-of-file	^Q ^C
	0501	0501	0509	Find string	^Q ^F

Table C-1. WS.COM Addresses For CP/M-80 Versions Of WordStar (Continued)

Label	3.3 DOS	3.0 CP/M-80	3.3 CP/M-80	Function	
	0505	0505	050C	Find and replace	^Q ^A
	0509	0509	0511	Find misspelling	^Q ^L
	050D	050D	0515	Find and repl again	^L
	0511	0511	0519	Start scrolling down	^Q ^W
	0515	0515	051C	Start scrolling up	^Q ^Z
	0519	0519	0521	Scroll up a line	^Z
	051D	051D	0525	Scroll down a line	^W
	0521	0521	0529	Page down	^R
	0525	0525	052C	Page up	^C
	0529	0529	0531	Delete character left	Del
	052D	052D	0535	Alternate to above	^ –
	0531	0531	0539	Delete char at cursor	^G
	0535	0535	053C	Delete entire line	^Y
	0539	0539	0541	Del to begin of line	^QDel
	053D	053D	0545	Alternate to above	^Q ^ –
	0541	0541	0549	Delete to end-of-line	^Q ^Y
	0545	0545	054C	Delete word right	^T
	0549	0549	0551	Insert on-off	^V
	054D	054D	0555	Reform paragraph	^B
	0551	0551	0559	Repeat next command	^Q ^Q
	0555	0555	055C	Insert blank line	^N
	0559	0559	0561	Tab right	^I
	055D	055D	0565	CR with LF	^M
	0561	0561	0569	Print menu prefix	^P
	0565	0565	056C	Hide/display mkd text	^K ^H
	0569	0569	0571	Mark block beginning	^KB
	056D	056D	0575	Mark block end	^KK
	0571	0571	0579	Set/hide marker zero	^K0
	0575	0575	057C	Set/hide marker one	^K1
	0579	0579	0581	Set/hide marker two	^K2
	057D	057D	0585	Set/hide marker three	^K3
	0581	0581	0589	Set/hide marker four	^K4
	0585	0585	058D	Set/hide marker five	^K5
	0589	0589	0591	Set/hide marker six	^K6
	058D	058D	0595	Set/hide marker seven	^K7
	0591	0591	0599	Set/hide marker eight	^K8
	0595	0595	059D	Set/hide marker nine	^K9
	0599	0599	05A1	Move marked text	^K ^V
	059D	059D	05A5	Copy marked text	^K ^C
	05A1	05A1	05A9	Delete marked text	^K ^Y
	05A5	05A5	05AD	Col block mode on/off	^K ^N
	05A9	05A9	05B1	(blank)	^K ^Z

Table C-1. WS.COM Addresses For CP/M-80 Versions Of WordStar (Continued)

Label	*3.3 DOS*	*3.0 CP/M-80*	*3.3 CP/M-80*	*Function*	
	05AD	05AD	05B5	Interrupt	^U
	05B1	05B1	05B9	Save file and exit	^K ^X
	05B5	05B5	05BD	Save, done editing	^K ^D
	05B9	05B9	05C1	Save-resume editing	^K ^S
	05BD	05BD	05C5	Abandon edit	^K ^Q
	05C1	05C1	05C9	Read file into text	^K ^R
	05C5	05C5	05CD	Write mkd blk to file	^K ^W
	05C9	05C9	05D1	Delete a file	^K ^J
	05CD	05CD	05D5	File directory on/off	^K ^F
	05D1	05D1	05D9	Print a file	^K ^P
	05D5	05D5	05DD	Change logged disk	^K ^L
	05D9	05D9	05E1	Copy a file	^K ^O
	05DD	05DD	05E5	Rename a file	^K ^E
	05E1	05E1	05E9	Set left margin	^O ^L
	05E5	05E5	05ED	Set right margin	^O ^R
	05E9	05E9	05F1	Set tab stop	^O ^I
	05ED	05ED	05F5	Clear tab stops	^O ^N
	05F1	05F1	05F9	Set mar/tabs fm text	^O ^F
	05F5	05F5	05FD	Word wrap on/off	^O ^W
	05F9	05F9	0601	Justification on/off	^O ^J
	05FD	05FD	0605	Variable tabs on/off	^O ^V
	0601	0601	0609	Hide/displ pnt ctrls	^O ^D
	0605	0605	060D	Rlr line displ on/off	^O ^T
	0609	0609	0611	Pg-brk displ on/off	^O ^P
	060D	060D	0615	Soft hyphens on/off	^O ^E
	0611	0611	0619	Hyphen-help on/off	^O ^H
	0615	0615	061D	Paragraph tab	^O ^G
	0619	0619	0621	Margin release	^O ^X
	061D	061D	0625	Center line	^O ^C
	0621	0621	0629	Set line spacing	^O ^S
	0625	0625	062D	Explain dot commands	^J ^D
	0629	0629	0631	Explain status line	^J ^S
	062D	062D	0635	Expl right-side flags	^J ^F
	0631	0631	0639	Explain place markers	^J ^P
	0635	0635	063D	Expl paragraph reform	^J ^B
	0639	0639	0641	Expl margins and tabs	^J ^M
	063D	063D	0645	Displ index of cmnds	^J ^I
	0641	0641	0649	Explain moving text	^J ^V
	0645	0645	064D	Explain ruler line	^J ^R
	n/a	n/a	0651		^J ^A

Table C-1. WS.COM Addresses For CP/M-80 Versions Of WordStar (Continued)

Label	3.3 DOS	3.0 CP/M-80	3.3 CP/M-80	Function	
			* * * Merge-Print Commands * * *		
FPTAB	0724	066E	067A	Pause-resume printing	^P
	0728	0672	067E	Scroll directory up	^Z
	072C	0676	0682	Scroll directory down	^W
			* * * Pointers And Special Characters * * *		
PNFPTAB	0735	067F	068B	Pointer to NOFTAB	
PVTAB	0737	0681	068D	Pointer to VTAB	
PFPTAB	0739	0683	068F	Pointer to FPTAB	
CLCHR	073C	0686	0691	Delete char left	^S
CRCHR	073D	0687	0692	Cursor right char	^D
LITCHR	073E	0688	0693	Take char literally	^P
DIRCH	073F	0689	0694	Turn dir on if off	^F
	0740	068A	0695	Scroll dir up	^Z
	0741	068B	0696	Scroll dir down	^W
STPCHR	0742	068C	0697	Interrupt character	^U
ERELCH	0743	068D	0698	Error release char	Esc
			* * * Printer Control Functions * * *		
POSMTH	0746	0690	0699	Specifies printer type	——
BLDSTR	0747	0691	069A	Num strikes for bold	^PB
DBLSTR	0748	0692	069B	Num strikes for dbl	^PD
PSCRLF	074C	0696	069C	Carriage Ret, LF	——
PSCR	0757	06A1	06A7	Carriage Ret, null	——
PSHALF	075E	06A8	06AE	For CR, half LF	——
PBACKS	0765	06AF	06B5	Printer backspace char	——
PALT	076B	06B5	06BB	Select alt pitch	^PA
PSTD	0770	06BA	06C0	Return to std pitch	^PN
ROLUP	0775	06BF	06C5	Roll for superscript	^PQ
ROLDOW	077A	06C4	06CA	Roll for subscript	^PV
USR1	077F	06C9	06CF	User selectable #1	^PQ
USR3	0789	06D3	06D9	User selectable #3	^PE
USR4	078E	06D8	06DE	User selectable #4	^PR
RIBBON	0793	06DD	06E3	Select alt ribbon	^PY
RIBOFF	0798	06E2	06E8	Reset ribbon color	^PY
PSINIT	079D	06E7	06ED	Printer init string	——
PSFINI	07AE	06F8	06FE	Printer ending string	——
SOCHR	07C1	070B	070F	Strike-out char (–)	^PX
ULCHR	07C2	070C	0710	Underline char (_)	^PS

Table C-1. WS.COM Addresses For CP/M-80 Versions Of WordStar (Continued)

Label	*3.3 DOS*	*3.0 CP/M-80*	*3.3 CP/M-80*	*Function*	
PRINIT	07C3	070D	0711	Not used for IBM PC	
PRFINI	07C6	0710	0714	" " " "	
CSWTCH	07C9	0717	0717	Selects printer driver	——
HAVBSY	07CA	0718	0718	FF if spl bsy rtn avail	——
PROTCL	0879	0786	0778	Protocol, serial only	——
EAKBSZ	087A	0787	0779	Applies if PROTCL = 1	——
DVMILE	087C	0790	077A	VMI Lead-in sequence	——
DVMITR	0881	n/a	077F	VMI Trailer; NEC 3550	——
DVMMIN	0886	0795	0784	VMI Minimum	——
DVMRNG	0888	0797	0786	VMI Range + 1	——
DHMILE	088A	0799	0788	HMI Lead-in sequence	——
DHMIFG	088F	079E	078D	HMI Flag; FF for 60ths	——
DHMIN	0890	079F	078E	HMI Minimum	——
DHRNG	0892	07A1	0790	HMI Range + 1	——
DFWD	0894	07A3	0792	Print forward	——
DBAK	0899	07A8	0797	Print backward	——
DSP	089E	07AD	079C	Daisy space	——
DBS	08A3	07B2	07A1	Daisy backspace	——
DLF	08A8	07B7	07A6	Daisy line feed	——
DRLF	08AD	07BC	07AB	Daisy reverse LF	——
DPHSPC	08B2	07C1	07B0	Print spl char	^PF
DPHRUB	08B6	07C5	07B4	Print alt spl char	^PG
				* * * Proportional Spacing Parameters * * *	
DNPROS	08C4	07D3	07B8	Suppress proport spacing	——
DMJWB	08C5	07D4	07B9	Alt microjustify algor.	——
PSTAB	08C9	07D8	07BA	Proport. spacing table	
	0928	0838	0828	End of WS.COM patch area	

Table C-2. Proportional Spacing Table Addresses For CP/M-80 Versions

Ver 3.0	*Ver 3.3*	*Val*	*Char*	*Ver 3.0*	*Ver 3.3*	*Val*	*Char*
07D8	07BA	52	ph spc	0808	07EA	53	P
07D9	07BB	43	!	0809	07EB	56	Q
07DA	07BC	44	"	080A	07EC	56	R
07DB	07BD	54	#	080B	07ED	54	S
07DC	07BE	54	$	080C	07EE	55	T
07DD	07BF	56	%	080D	07EF	56	U
07DE	07C0	56	&	080E	07F0	56	V
07DF	07C1	32	'	080F	07F1	67	W
07E0	07C2	43	(	0810	07F2	56	X
07E1	07C3	43	)	0811	07F3	56	Y
07E2	07C4	54	*	0812	07F4	55	Z
07E3	07C5	54	+	0813	07F5	54	[
07E4	07C6	42	,	0814	07F6	56	\
07E5	07C7	54	–	0815	07F7	54	]
07E6	07C8	32	.	0816	07F8	56	^
07E7	07C9	53	/	0817	07F9	55	_
07E8	07CA	54	0	0818	07FA	54	`
07E9	07CB	54	1	0819	07FB	54	a
07EA	07CC	54	2	081A	07FC	54	b
07EB	07CD	54	3	081B	07FD	54	c
07EC	07CE	54	4	081C	07FE	54	d
07ED	07CF	54	5	081D	07FF	54	e
07EE	07D0	54	6	081E	0800	53	f
07EF	07D1	54	7	081F	0801	54	g
07F0	07D2	54	8	0820	0802	54	h
07F1	07D3	54	9	0821	0803	53	i
07F2	07D4	43	:	0822	0804	52	j
07F3	07D5	42	;	0823	0805	54	k
07F4	07D6	54	<	0824	0806	52	l
07F5	07D7	54	=	0825	0807	66	m
07F6	07D8	54	>	0826	0808	54	n
07F7	07D9	54	?	0827	0809	54	o
07F8	07DA	56	@	0828	080A	54	p
07F9	07DB	55	A	0829	080B	54	q
07FA	07DC	55	B	082A	080C	53	r
07FB	07DD	55	C	082B	080D	53	s
07FC	07DE	56	D	082C	080E	53	t
07FD	07DF	55	E	082D	080F	54	u
07FE	07E0	55	F	082E	0810	54	v
07FF	07E1	56	G	082F	0811	66	w
0800	07E2	56	H	0830	0812	54	x
0801	07E3	53	I	0831	0813	54	y
0802	07E4	53	J	0832	0814	54	z
0803	07E5	56	K	0833	0815	54	{
0804	07E6	55	L	0834	0816	56	|
0805	07E7	66	M	0835	0817	54	}
0806	07E8	56	N	0836	0818	56	~
0807	07E9	56	O	0837	0819	55	ph rub

Appendix D

COMPUTER TERMS AND CRYPTICISMS

It is impossible to discuss or read about computers and software for long without running into terms peculiar to the subject—and often peculiar in any sense. The field is riddled with jargon, some of it borrowed from general language and occasionally corrupted, much of it coined to fit a discipline whose natural idiom sits uncomfortably astride language needs of both humans and machines. It should come as no surprise, therefore, that the result is often a curious but practical amalgam.

Most of its lexical excesses are innocuous, many even whimsical, but some are enough to send a shudder through those who care about language. The terminology has become so widely used and accepted, however, that any attempt to set things right would do little more than impede communication. Meanwhile, its perpetrators charge blithely onward, focused not on finer points of language but on simply getting the job done.

With a sometimes rueful nod to pragmatism, here is a short compendium of terms used in this book. Definitions are consistent with general field usage but in some cases are tilted toward a WordStar context.

Address A unique identifier of the place where an item of data is located. Can be expressed directly and absolutely, as in a hexadecimal memory location, or indirectly in the form of a label. Also called a starting address if involving several items, such as a table.

Algorithm A procedure, usually internal and expressed mathematically or logically, specifying how a certain group or class of data is to be handled or a certain task is to be done. Example: rules and procedures governing justification of lines in WordStar.

Application A program or class of programs designed for some end task such as accounting, engineering, word processing, etc., as opposed to programs necessary for basic operation of a computer, such as operating systems. WordStar is an application program; DOS is not.

ASCII American Standard Code For Information Interchange. A defined set of 256 characters including alphabetic letters, numerals, punctuation, and special characters, each having a unique numeric equivalent. Values may be expressed in decimal, hexadecimal, or binary. Normal printing characters are included in the first 128, a common subset being 96 characters.

Binary The most elemental number system used by computers, consisting of only two units, 1 and 0, called bits. Operations at the basic machine level are in binary, since the digital electronic circuits of which a computer is built have only two operating states: on or off, equivalent to one and zero. (See Appendix A for more on its relationship to other systems.)

Bit A contraction of *Bi*nary digi*t*. Unit of the binary number system and the smallest element of data used in computing systems. Has only two forms or states: 1 and 0. Used in groupings to form higher orders of data, such as bytes.

Boot Also bootstrap, from the expression, "Lifting yourself up by your own bootstraps." A process whereby a computer's operating system starts and loads itself one piece at a time, using previously loaded sections to load and execute following sections, ultimately reaching full operating status. Also used to clear memory and reload a program after making a patch.

Buffer A temporary storage area, often involving various kinds of memory devices. Frequently used as a data staging area between units operating at widely different speeds, such as a processor and a printer, so that the faster unit is not continuously tied up by the slower unit.

Byte A data form consisting of a series of 8 bits. Origin thought to be from bite, as in "a bite of data." Can represent a numeric value of up to 255 decimal or FF hexadecimal, or any of the 256 ASCII characters (first of which is a null, or no character).

Code As a collective noun, the individual instructions comprising a program. As a verb, the actual writing of instructions as opposed to the planning and designing aspects of programming. Can also mean a symbolic representation of some other quantity.

Default A specified value or operating condition to which a program reverts in the absence of an instruction to the contrary (i.e., the normal value or state, as in "10-pitch" or "On"). Also used as a verb.

Dump As a verb, to display or print the exact data contents of a storage unit, such as memory, so that it can be examined, modified, or retained as a record. As a noun, the displayed or printed output.

Field An area reserved for a specified class of data, such as a label, an entry specifying the length of a related record, etc. It can be of fixed or variable length; most we deal with in WordStar are fixed.

File A stored collection of records characterized by an external name or label. May consist of data, text, or programs.

Flag A short record, usually one or two bytes (can be as short as one bit), which alerts a program to some condition, such as an error, or causes it to divert in some way from its usual operation. Depending on the type of flag and its purpose, it can be set on or off automatically by the program or be set externally, usually remaining in the set position until changed.

Hexadecimal Combination of the Greek prefix hexa, meaning six, and decimal, or ten, producing sixteen. A numbering system used with computers and having a base of 16. (See Appendix A for more details.)

High-Order Bit The left-most bit in a byte. The normal printing subset of the ASCII character set uses only seven bits. WordStar uses the remaining, or high-order, bit to mark the ends of words in formed paragraphs and for other special purposes.

Initialize To put in motion a sequence of start-up procedures, largely internal, which set a program to an initial condition or state of operation. A horrible corruption of language, but definitive in accepted meaning.

Interface A term tossed about freely and loosely as both a noun and a verb. In a technical sense it refers to the interconnection—physical, electrical, or functional—between any two elements of a system. The term often implies some level of specification common to both sides to ensure compatibility. (See also Protocol.)

Label A name, often limited to eight characters, usually identifying a specific field, table, routine or subroutine, or other function within a program. Depending on size of the label field and the care taken by the programmer, labels can provide clues to the purposes of associated program functions. They are also used internally to enable the program to find elements that are moved during program operation and therefore do not have fixed addresses.

Logic Refers in a general sense to the arrangement, nature, and sequence of instructions responsible for executing program functions, as opposed to the constants, fixed and variable, and other data used by these instructions as the program executes. Also refers to digital electronic circuit elements.

Literal A value to be used by the program as it stands, such as a number indicating the number of lines per page or an alphabetic character displayed in a message or menu. (See also Symbolic.)

Nibble (also Nybble) What else but half a byte? Four bits.

Overlay A section of a program not normally residing in memory but called in from another storage medium, such as disk, when needed. It is written into memory on top of whatever previously occupied the space. Its purpose is to reduce working memory space needed by a program, leaving more space available for data, such as text files. When its task is completed, the main program may call and rewrite the original program section into memory.

Patch Refers to a technique for modifying a program by operating directly on its machine-executable form, as opposed to changing the source code produced by the programmer when the program was written. Its main advantage is that it can be done quickly and does not require access to the original instructions if appropriate memory addresses are known. A drawback is that it requires working with individual bytes expressed in usually unfamiliar form and is therefore more error-prone.

Protocol A set of technical ground rules and conventions, usually formally defined, specifying how operations are to be conducted. Most frequently applied to communication links, where it usually relates to procedures for establishing, maintaining, and terminating connections.

RAM An abbreviation for Random Access Memory. Specifically refers to the semiconductor integrated-circuit devices (popularly but imprecisely known as chips) commonly used for the main memory in personal computers and as data storage elements in modern printers. Also used to refer generally to any form of storage using such devices.

Record A general form of reference to data, usually meaning data stored in some permanent medium and often in some predetermined format. Records often contain fields and can be of any size within system limits. A collection of records given an external name becomes a file.

Routine A set of instructions which performs some particular task, often repetitive in nature, within the program as a whole. Also general reference to sections of a program, as in "input routines." (See also Subroutine.)

Software Collectively the programs that render a computer capable of doing useful work, as in loading and executing application programs. Included are operating systems, communication programs, input/output programs, device handlers such as printer drivers, etc. Broadly speaking, all programs are software. Also used in apposition to equipment, then referring to all parts of a system that are not hardware.

Subroutine A set of program instructions which perform a specific function, such as calculating some value and storing it for use by another part of the program. Distinction from a routine is somewhat arbitrary.

Symbolic An indirect form of expression in which the data or value present stands for something else and is not used directly by a program in that form. A label, for example, can be a symbolic form of an address.

Table A series of related data, usually organized into some uniform format, which the program often must access frequently. Often used for both fixed and variable data which establish values for various operating parameters. WordStar contains numerous tables of varied sizes.

Toggle A function which is set alternately on and off by its controlling mechanism. WordStar examples are ^B (boldface), ^S (underline), etc.

Utility Refers to a broad class of general purpose programs which usually do some specialized task in support of a larger activity. Examples are sorting, filing, printing, file maintenance, and the like.

Index

AN INVITATION TO READERS.

It is hoped by both author and publisher that you have found this book useful, accurate, and complete. As future versions of WordStar are released, periodic updates of the book are planned through new editions. In this way we hope to continue providing you with the most comprehensive, up-to-date guidebook and reference available on WordStar customizing.

We invite your participation in achieving this objective. If you have comments or suggestions for improvement, or if you have discovered a useful aspect of WordStar customizing not covered here, send your inputs to the author in care of Wordware, 1506 Capital Avenue, Plano, TX 75074. All inputs will be welcome, and substantial contributions will be acknowledged in future editions.

THE COMPUTER PROFESSIONAL SERIES

For the corporate and MIS business professional involved in systems management of micro, mini, or mainframe computers. Networking, applications development technologies, and telecommunications are among the technical subjects featured.

THE FOCUS DEVELOPERS HANDBOOK

BART BENNE

This advanced book on FOCUS provides answers to questions about systems design, file maintenance, reporting, graphics, statistics, and security considerations.

Techniques taught in this innovative book improve the productivity level of FOCUS users, allowing development of complete applications in a fraction of the time required with COBOL or other languages.

VISIT YOUR LOCAL BOOK STORE TODAY!
If these books are not available, contact Wordware Publishing, Inc.
CALL TOLL FREE 1-800-231-7467